On Your Bike in Surrey

Valerie Bennett

Photographs by James Bennett

COUNTRYSIDE BOOKS
NEWBURY BERKSHIRE

First published 2001

Revised and updated 2002

COUNTRYSIDE BOOKS
3 Catherine Road
Newbury, Berkshire

To view our complete range of books,
please visit us at
www.countrysidebooks.co.uk

ISBN 1 85306 663 X

Designed by Graham Whiteman
Maps by Gelder design and mapping

Produced through MRM Associates Ltd., Reading
Printed in Italy

CONTENTS

AREA MAP SHOWING THE LOCATIONS OF THE RIDES

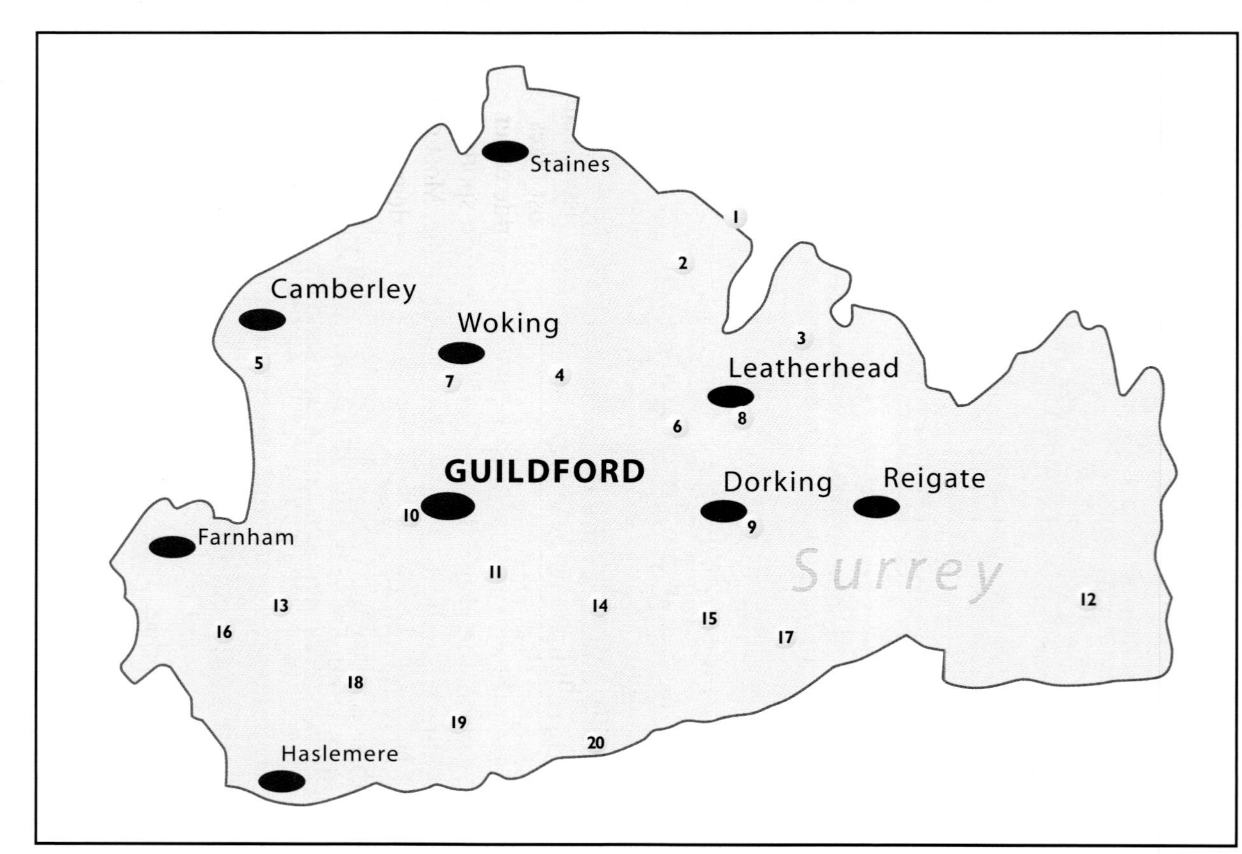

INTRODUCTION

This book should help you to explore some areas of Surrey that you may not have known existed. You can cover ground quickly on a bicycle but you can also stop and look at whatever attracts your attention, be it an historic building, wildlife or a river scene. I have discovered some wonderful places in Surrey whilst researching these routes and hope that you, too, will enjoy the exhilaration and adventure of exploring new places on two wheels in the changing seasons.

The purpose of the book is to offer a guide to all leisure cyclists and to families. It is also intended to encourage both those new to cycling and those who are apprehensive about returning to it. The routes offer a saunter through beautiful country with the opportunity to stop and see places of interest, to rest at a pub or sit and soak up the atmosphere. The rides vary in length from 14 miles to 23 miles. You will probably want to take your time to enjoy these routes fully and take a break for lunch at one of the pubs or tearooms on the way. With the help of a map you can shorten or lengthen the rides. You can cycle along the Thames Path from Hampton Court, for example, and return by ferry from Kingston.

The aim has been to find circular routes with a minimum of steep hills on quiet roads, easy bridleways and river towpaths. Most lie within Surrey whilst two or three extend just over the border into Sussex, Hampshire and Richmond. These routes should be suitable for most bikes although using a bike with at least some gears will make your ride easier and the off-road sections are likely to preclude the lightweight sports variety. Don't dismiss riding a bike because of concerns about traffic. Most of each route is quiet. There are usually only short stretches with a degree of traffic and where there is a busy road there is often a pavement where you can get off and push your bike.

Remember that cycling is not only fun but is also good for you. The British Medical Association's report *Cycling: Towards Health and Safety* points out that cycling regularly will improve your fitness and can help you to live a long and healthy life.

Have some wonderful adventures in the Surrey countryside.

Valerie Bennett

GUIDE TO USING THIS BOOK

Each route is preceded by information to help you:

The **number of miles** is the total that you will cover excluding detours.

The brief **introduction** to the ride gives a broad picture of where the route goes and also mentions particular features you will see.

Using a **map** in conjunction with these routes is highly recommended. Ordnance Survey Landranger (1¼ inches to 1 mile) should provide all the information that you need. OS Explorer maps (2½ inches to 1 mile) will offer even more detail.

The grid reference of the suggested **starting point** is given. You can start from any convenient location on the route. Where a pub car park is suggested the landlord has already given permission in principle for readers to park. However, all landlords ask that you telephone or ask when parking in case the pub has a special function. They will appreciate it if you patronise their pubs if only for a drink.

There is a leaflet called *Cycling by Train* available from the Cyclists Touring Club (telephone: 01483 417217) or telephone South West Trains (023 8021 3600) for information. The nearest **station**(s) to the route has been given. Use a map to reach the route from the station of your choice.

The names of pubs and tearooms for **refreshment** are given as a guide. Many of these have been sampled and enjoyed. However, it has not been possible to sample every establishment and landlords and menus change frequently so try other pubs or cafés that attract you as well. Remember that the Highway Code states that you must not ride under the influence of drink or drugs.

An indication is given about **how level the route is**. In general those that run near rivers and canals and the Downs Link are the most level. Most of the routes in this book are planned so that they avoid the steepest hills in the North Downs and are not too difficult. Only one or two rides have long substantial hills and these are indicated within the boxes.

THE ROUTES

It is a good idea to read right through a route before setting out so that you note any places where you want to spend more time. The directions have been written as clearly as possible. Instructions to change direction are written in bold type, ie **turn R**. Instructions to continue straight on are not in bold.

At the end of each route there is more information about **places of interest**. These include notes about architecture, history and people connected with each entry.

Some routes are in, around or pass through **urban areas**, eg Epsom, Esher, Guildford and Richmond. They are included because there are quiet and varied cycleways through the areas and they offer a taster of some of the exciting developments in cycling routes. Ingenious routes away from traffic need to be more detailed so be prepared to take more time. Use the Epsom and Richmond routes in conjunction with free cycling guide maps. Consider marking the route from this book on the map before setting out and on your ride refer back to the text at problem spots.

It is possible to use maps to **shorten or extend** most rides so try experimenting. Routes 10, 13 and 16 share short sections. You can almost double the length of the ride by adding route number 13 to route number 16 with the aid of a map. Routes 9 and 17 may be treated in the same way.

Be prepared to get off and **push your bike** for short distances along footpaths where cycling is not allowed and, on one or two routes, up steps to cross bridges.

SAFETY

There are many common sense dos and don'ts. The Cyclists' Tourist Club offers a comprehensive *Get into Cycle Touring Basics* leaflet and also a specialised service for the leisure cyclist for everything you need from buying a bike to insurance (telephone: 01483 417217, or contact them at www.ctc.org.uk).

Ensure that your bike is roadworthy and in particular that brakes and gears are in good working order and tyres are in good condition. Take a spare inner tube or a puncture repair kit with you and the tools. If you cannot change an inner tube or repair a puncture then have a strategy for dealing with the eventuality. Consider taking a padlock in case you park your bike to explore an area.

Always be in control of your bike. Ride on the quietest of lanes as though a car is approaching. It may be. Off-road there may be the unexpected root, pedestrian or horserider ahead. Either fit your bike with a bell or call out if necessary to alert pedestrians and horseriders that you are behind them.

Wear comfortable bright or light coloured clothing to ensure that you are seen. You are advised to wear shoes that will cope with mud. You may need to push your bike on a footpath and even the best of off-road routes can have the odd muddy patch after rain and in winter. Make sure that you have no loose or dangling clothing that could get tangled in the wheel or chain.

Wearing a helmet is advisable particularly for children. There is plenty of literature available on the subject.

It would be advisable to take water, food and perhaps a good breathable waterproof jacket.

Although not essential, a cycle computer is very useful for measuring distances and it will help you with the route.

There are some wonderful places to see and cycling offers a unique way of seeing them. Enjoy it.

ACKNOWLEDGEMENTS

I would like to acknowledge the help given by the officers of the Borough Councils of Epsom, Esher and Guildford. Much of the credit for the Around the Hog's Back route goes to Martin Taplin, a member of the Guildford Cycle Group. The off-road guide maps published by Oaktree Routes have saved me cycling many a mile along unsuitable bridleways. Lastly to Anne Mustoe whose books about her amazing round the world travels on her bicycle served as an inspiration to get on my bike in the first place, albeit in Surrey.

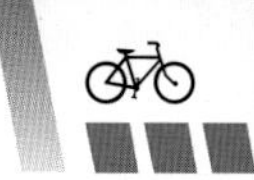

1

Hampton Court and Richmond Park

20 miles

From Bushy Park it is not far to Hampton Court Palace to join a section of the National Cycle Network along the Thames Path. Savour the sights and scenes of the river, linger at Ham House, a National Trust property, and have lunch at a table on the Orangery lawn. Then experience cycle-friendly Richmond Park with its extensive parkland, herds of deer and ponds, where you can explore the gardens and terrace at Pembroke Lodge and see wonderful views of London. Return via splendid Teddington Lock and past Teddington Film Studios to Bushy Park.

Map: OS Landranger 176 West London (GR 160694). Guides entitled *Cycling in Richmond-upon-Thames* and *Cycling in Richmond Park* available free from Richmond Tourist Information, telephone: 020 8940 9125. Refer to **urban areas** in the guide at the front of the book.

Starting point: The car park near the Diana Fountain in Bushy Park. From Hampton Court take the A308 in the direction of Twickenham. In 250 yards turn left through the gateway into the Park. Drive to the roundabout, take the second exit and the car park is shortly on the left.

By train: Hampton Court station is just the other side of the Thames from the route.

Refreshments: The Boatman pub is north of Kingston, and in Ham Street there is the Brewery Tap. National Trust fare is available at Ham House – remember to take your National Trust membership card with you. In Richmond Park and at Pembroke Lodge are refreshment vans, and there are also pubs on the far side of Teddington Lock.

The route: This is level riding. You cycle on the Thames Path and on cycle paths in Richmond Park. Where there are roads they are either quiet, traffic-calmed or have pavements where you can push your bike.

Turn L from the car park onto Chestnut Avenue. **Turn R** out of the park gates onto the A308 for ⅓ mile. **Turn L** along the Thames Path just past the entrance to Hampton Court Palace. Ride past the splendid gates of the Palace where Tudor kings and queens would have entered from the Thames. Later you pass Raven's Ait, an island sailing school.

Turn R at Kingston Bridge, cross the bridge following the Thames Cycle Route signs. Ride along the cycle path

on the right-hand bank of the river. Take a break at the Boaters Inn and watch all the life of the river. The path joins a quiet road but soon **bear L** by a sign indicating the Thames Path. Cycle along the gravelled Thames route for about a mile.

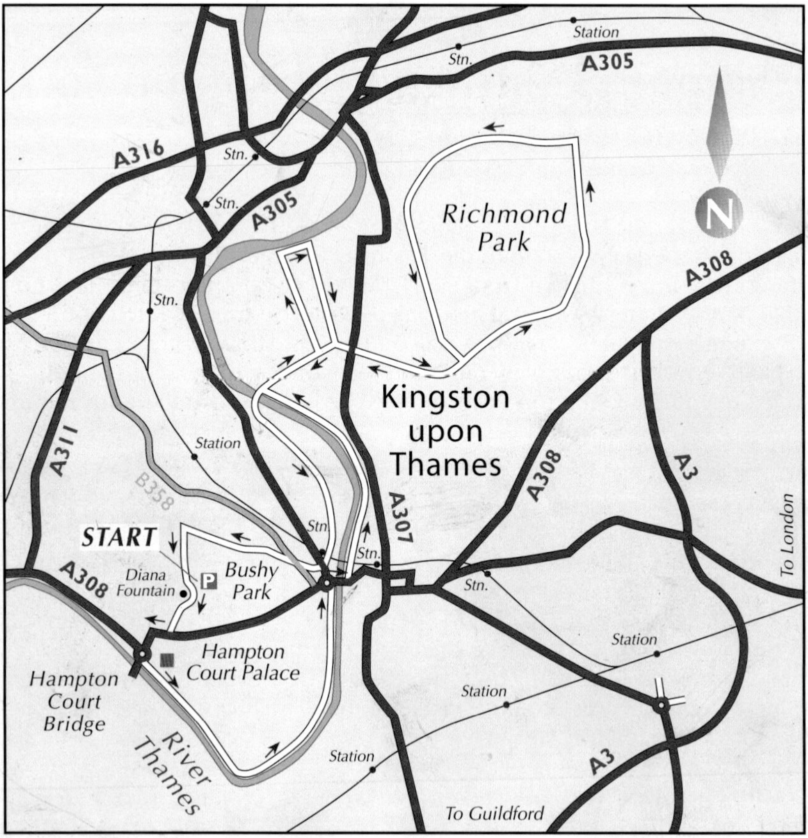

Turn R along a paved path immediately before Teddington Lock in the direction of Richmond Park. Ride across Riverside Road and straight ahead into a passageway between the fenced gardens of houses. Cross Hardwicke Road, go straight along another passageway and then **turn R** into Broughton Avenue. **Turn L** in a few yards into Lock Road in the direction of Ham Common.

In less than ½ mile **turn L** along Ham Street in the direction of Ham House. The road winds on towards the river and Ham House is on the right near to the end. If you are a National Trust member or are prepared to pay the entrance fee, leave time to park your bike and have a look at the mansion or stroll around the gardens. The tearoom menu is irresistible and to eat at a table on the Orangery Lawn is a delight. It is an outstanding Stuart house and there is a 17th-century formal garden and rare collections of furniture and paintings in the house.

Return to Ham Street and in about 100

Looking across the Thames to Hampton Court Palace

yards you reach a car park and the river. There are views to Eel Pie Island and Richmond Hill. **Turn R** along the path and shortly the landing stage of Hammerton's Foot Ferry is on your left. **Turn R** opposite this along a narrow path signposted to Ham House. Keep to the left of the house and follow the track which is called Melancholy Walk. At a T-junction of paths **turn R**. Then follow the path back to Ham, crossing Sandy Lane. **Turn L** in the direction of Richmond Park.

Cross the A307 at the traffic lights. Ride along Ham Gate Avenue and through the gates into Richmond Park. Join the gravelled track to the left of the road and climb the hill. Cross the road at the top and ride straight on between grassy verges. In about a mile **turn L** at the T-junction. There is a car park on your left where there is a van selling food and drinks. There are picnic tables where you can sit and relax and Pen Ponds are visible in the distance.

Continue along the pathway past the turning to White Lodge, the Royal Ballet School. There is a good downhill run towards the roundabout but mind the ramps. Use the cycle path on the right and cross straight over the road. At Sheen Gate **turn L** following the cycle track round the park past Cambrian Gate and Richmond Gate. At Pembroke Lodge there are attractive gardens, refreshments and splendid views across London from the terrace.

Return to the cycle path which runs parallel to the road. At an intersection **turn R** along the steeply descending cycle path towards Ham Gate where you entered the park. Ride back along

Ham Gate Avenue, over the traffic lights and past Ham. Retrace the route along Lock Road, **turn R** into Broughton Avenue and in a few yards **turn L** along the passageways back to Teddington Lock following the blue signs.

Cross over Teddington Lock using the cycle channels for your bike. As you cross the suspension bridge you will notice the splendid lock and weirs. From Ferry Road **turn first L** into Broom Road. Soon to your left is Teddington Studios with its blue plaques to commemorate the stars of well-known British film and TV productions. Ride to the end of the road and **turn R** into Hampton Wick High Street. **Turn L** soon into Park Road and cycle to the end. **Turn R** into Sandy Lane. **Turn L** into Bushy Park at the next gate immediately before the road bends to the right. Notice the memorial to Timothy Bennet, the shoemaker. Ride along Cobbler's Walk and **turn L** into Chestnut Avenue. The car park is about ½ mile on your left.

HAMPTON COURT PALACE

Henry VIII was passionate about his palace by the Thames, which was built over 500 years ago. There are six acres of buildings including Henry VIII's State Apartments, the Georgian Rooms where a sound guide describes the private world of George II and Queen Caroline, and the Tudor Kitchens and much, much more. The 60 acres of gardens include the great maze. You can push your bike through the gardens and along the terrace to the riverside without charge.

COBBLER'S WALK

There is a memorial to Timothy Bennet just outside Bushy Park at the start of Cobbler's Path. He was an 18th-century shoemaker who was determined to fight the closure of the path through Bushy Park. He believed that the world should not be left worse off than he had found it so he decided to take the matter to court and spend the considerable sum of £700 on the legal costs. Lord Halifax feared public defeat and withdrew. The walk, called Cobbler's Walk, exists to this day and extends from Hampton Wick to Hampton Hill.

2

Esher, Thames Ditton and Sunbury

17½ miles

This ride, starting within a stone's throw of Esher, offers woodland and riverside beauty on Surrey's northernmost boundary. Explore the wooded trails of Esher Common, use bridleways to weave over, under and around the A3 and ride along the Thames Path from Hampton Court to Walton. You pass Molesey and Sunbury Locks, Garrick's temple can be seen on the north bank and swans and Canada geese at Hurst Park. The Thames hums with activity. A pub, the Weir near Sunbury, provides a welcome break where you can gaze at the river and the water rushing through the weir. Return by roads through Walton and back to the countryside of West End Common. Make a detour and cross the Thames to visit magnificent Hampton Court Palace on the way.

Map: OS Landranger 176 West London (GR 125627).

Starting point: Horseshoe Clump car park, West End Common, opposite Blackhills Road, ¼ mile south of Claremont Landscape Garden, Esher on the A307.

By train: Hampton Court and Thames Ditton stations are both within yards of the route.

Refreshments: Try the Weir, the Anglers, or the Swan near Sunbury Locks for refreshments. At Hampton Court there is plenty of choice. The Streets of London at Thames Ditton serves pizza.

The route: This is a comparatively flat route with a mixture of tracks, river towpath and roads. There is some urban riding between Sunbury and Esher but there are stretches of cycle lane and traffic-calmed roads. Refer to **urban areas** in the guide at the front of the book. Bike riding is yet to be negotiated on two short off-road sections of the route but a change of pace and pushing your bike can be a pleasure.

Cross the A307, **turn R** for a few yards in the direction of Cobham and then **L** along Esher Common Cycle Route following the white arrows. **Turn R** at the T-junction and **bear L** before reaching the A3. Ride along this wide track as it climbs towards the bridge and descends into woodland. (Do not cross the bridge.) Cycle for nearly a mile from the bridge along the signed path. Go through a gate and cross straight over the A244, a busy road, to the path opposite.

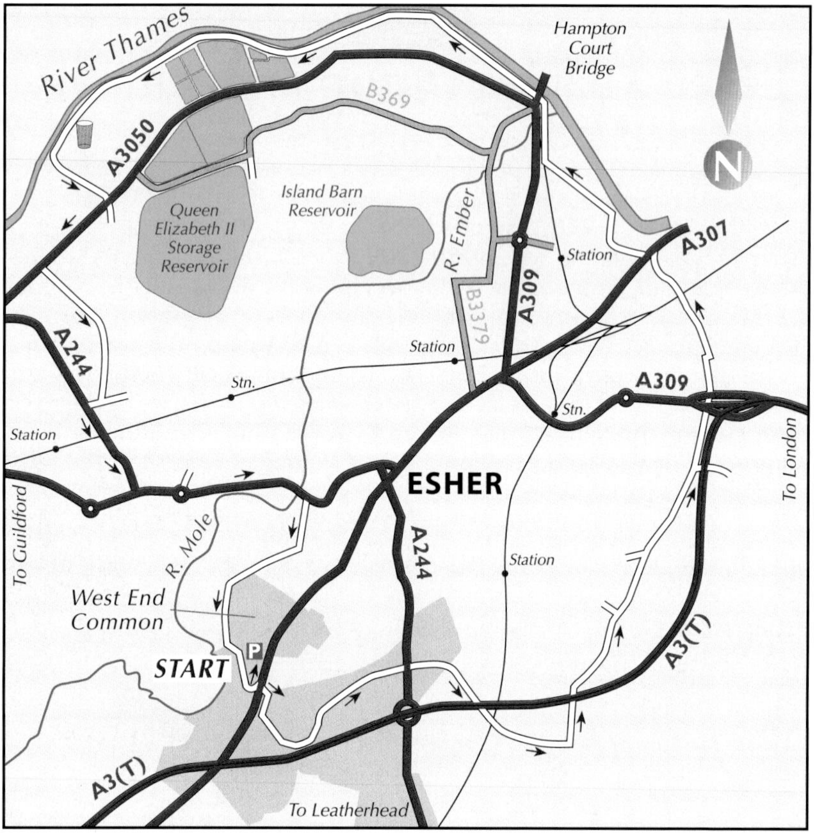

Ride on to a junction with a lane and **turn R** then immediately **L** following the bike trail.

In about 200 yards, where the path divides, **turn R** away from the bike route and take the horse ride marked with a blue arrow, signposted to Claygate. Cycle out of the woods and along the track passing open fields and through the A3 underpass.

Shortly **bear R** where the track divides and mud looms ahead. Go under the railway bridge and pedal for nearly ¾ mile to a wide crossing track where the route ahead is barred.

Turn L and ride up and over the A3. **Turn R** into Holroyd Road. In about 200 yards **turn L** along a horse ride with houses to the right of it onto Claygate Common. Cycling is not yet agreed so push your bike for ⅓ mile.

At a road junction **bear R** into Stevens Lane and ride up the hill. At the T-junction **turn R** into Woodstock Lane South.

In about ½ mile **turn L** towards Surbiton Golf Club. In ⅓ mile at 'No entry' signs **turn L** and walk under the underpass.

Cross over the road to the nursery and

Taking time out to watch the cricket

into Woodstock Lane North. Follow the road downhill (**bearing L** into Rectory Lane) to an offset crossroads. Ride on into Ewell Road and under the railway bridge to the Portsmouth Road traffic lights.

Turn L and move to the centre lane. **Turn R** immediately into St Leonard's Road. At a roundabout take the 2nd exit along Summer Road. Soon Ye Olde Swan pub is on your right where you can go down the slipway to see a peaceful spot on the Thames. Continue for ½ mile to the railway crossing and at the junction with the A309 **turn R** onto the cycle path.

At Hampton Court Station why not cross the bridge and visit Hampton Court Palace?

Return to the station and cross the A309 towards the Streets of London pub following the National Cycle Route, number 4. Ride along Riverbank as far as the memorial.

Cross over and ride onto the Thames towpath keeping by the river for nearly 4½ miles. Pass Molesey Lock and Hurst Park where you may see many swans and Canada geese. At Sunbury Lock push your bike as indicated. There are some beautiful river scenes and you may be tempted to just sit and look at life from the river bank. The Weir pub is about 11½ miles from the start and has beautiful views of the weir.

In 1 mile further at the Anglers pub **turn L** away from the towpath. **Turn L** at the Swan onto Manor Road and ride straight ahead at the mini roundabout.

At the T-junction **turn L** for about 200 yards along the busy A3050. At the mini roundabout **turn R** along Sydney Road for 1 mile. At the next mini-roundabout **turn R** onto Rydens Road.

At the traffic lights **turn L** onto the A244 Hersham Road. Cycle under the railway bridge in the direction of Esher.

In just over ½ mile **move in to the left** to the cycle track. **Turn L** with the track in the direction of Esher. Ride on the cycle track to the roundabout and go straight across using the crossing facility.

Follow the cycle lane for a mile to another roundabout. Take the 3rd exit into West End Lane past the Princess Alice Hospice.

Turn R past the Prince of Wales along Winterdown Road. The pond is on your left and soon you reach Garson Farm Stables. **Bear L** under the height barrier to West End Common.

Cycle on the track for about ¼ mile past woods and open fields to a 'no horses' sign. **Bear L** in front of this following the blue horse ride signs. You need to push your bike as cycling is not yet allowed. The ride curves right and then rises sharply.

Bear R at the top of the hill. Shortly there is a grassy clearing on your left. **Turn L** past a bench seat and the car park is a few yards ahead.

THAMES DITTON

This is a riverside village although it is only from the Olde Swan Inn with the small slipway that the Thames can be seen. The name of Ditton is thought to originate from 'dictun', farm by the dyke, when there were a farm and five manors in the area according to the Domesday Book. The village now has a network of narrow streets and has many interesting and picturesque small shops.

THE THAMES PATH

The Thames Path is a long distance path which follows the river for over 200 miles from its source in Gloucestershire to the Thames Barrier near Greenwich. The Path is part of the National Cycle Network promoted by Sustrans, the engineering charity. Sustrans is working with local authorities and others to achieve some 8,000 miles of signposted cycle routes throughout the UK by 2005. You sample 4½ miles of the National Cycle Network on the route.

3

Epsom Parks, Downs and Commons

16 miles

Epsom has a developing network of cycle routes and this semi-urban wander, much of it off-road, makes an unusual contrast. Weave your way along quiet streets and passageways, through residential areas and round town parks. Ride from Epsom Downs to Nonsuch Park and from Horton Country Park to Epsom Common. Enjoy Bourne Hall Park with its fountain, the old world charm of Ewell and stroll around the gardens at Nonsuch Mansion where you can indulge in a delicious snack in the coffee shop courtyard.

Maps: OS Landranger 187 Dorking and Reigate (GR 220587). Epsom and Ewell Cycle Guide: a useful map obtainable free from Epsom and Ewell Borough Council is strongly recommended (telephone: 01372 732000). Refer to **urban areas** in the guide at the front of the book.

Starting point: The car park on Grandstand Road close to the roundabout and Grandstand on Epsom Downs.

By train: Tattenham Corner and Epsom stations are both about 1 mile from the route.

Refreshments: Take your pick from the Derby Arms, Rubbing House and Tattenham Corner, all at Epsom Downs; the Amato pub, Chalk Lane and the Star, Ewell. Nonsuch Park Mansion coffee shop for delicious cakes, sandwiches and Italian ice cream.

The route: An easy ride with the exception of the steady climb to Epsom Downs. Most roads are quiet or traffic-calmed. Busy roads usually have designated crossing places. Shorten the route by riding around Horton Park and Epsom Common. Extend it by cycling the off-road cycle routes around the Downs which start near the Grandstand. Be prepared to follow more detailed directions as you weave around the Borough.

Start from the pedestrian lights on the Epsom side of the grandstand. Turn into the pathway beside the racecourse. The pathway slopes to join Chalk Lane. **Turn L** and cycle down the shaded hill. At Dundas Stables ride around the barrier and pass Chalk Lane Hotel.

At the end **turn R** before the Ladas pub into the wide pedestrian/cycle pathway. Cross Avenue Road and into the pathway to Rosebery Park. **Turn R** before reaching the duck pond and go over the park and the crossing.

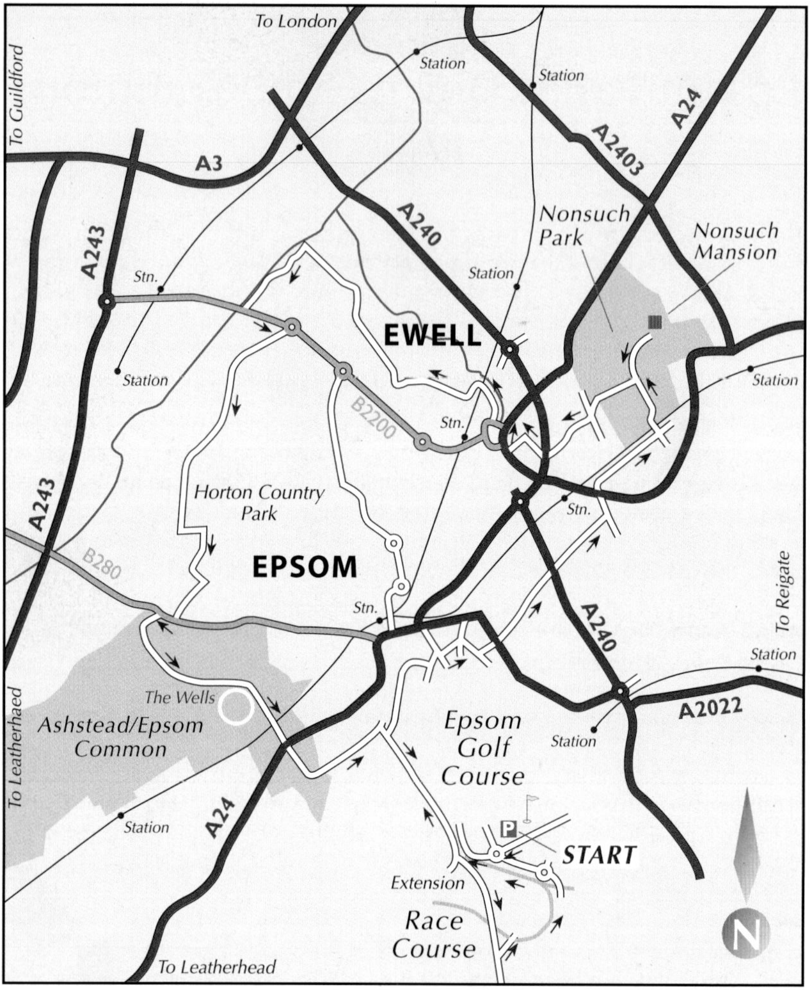

Ride into Heathcote Road. At the T-junction **turn L** into Worple Road. **Turn R** into Church Street and soon **L** into Grove Road. **Bear L** into Church Road and soon **R** into Albert Road.

Turn L into Bridle Road and cycle a straight, but frequently intersected, pathway for 1¼ miles. Ride up the hill past the allotments, along the cycle/pedestrian path, cross the road and ride straight ahead through Alexandra Recreation Ground. Your path ahead is hidden in the right-hand corner. Pass fenced gardens, school sports fields, cross residential roads and the A240. Then cycle the gravelled path past the fields of the College of Technology. Emerge with Kingdom Hall on your right.

Turn L into Banstead Road and **L** into Cheam Road. In a few yards cross the road and **turn R** into quiet

The large pond on Epsom Common

Queensmead Avenue. Ride up and over the hill. **Turn L** at the lowest point following the cycleway sign. Ride under the railway bridge and into Woodland Trust land. Cycle over the common, into the woods and across two concreted tracks. Enter Nonsuch Park and **turn L** at a T-junction of paths.

Immediately **turn R** to make a diversion to Nonsuch Mansion, gardens and the coffee house. Park your bike and wander around the mansion gardens where there are carpets of snowdrops in early spring. Rest at the coffee shop, a relaxing haven at any time of year. Return to the T-junction where you made the diversion and **turn R**.

Follow the path for ⅓ mile to the corner of the park. Leave the main path and ride ahead up the sloping pathway. Follow the narrow paved tree-lined path as it bends left. **Turn R** into Castle Avenue and **bear L** as it runs parallel to the bypass. Cross the A24 and turn into a narrow pathway off the layby. **Turn L** and then **R** into Ewell High Street.

A useful pedestrian crossing assists in the 200 yard walk to Bourne Hall which you enter through an elegant white gateway. Push your bike across the bridge and admire the spectacular fountain and bird life on the lake. Follow the lake around to the right where you will find a notice board with information about Bourne Hall. Continue past the board to leave the park by the gateway.

Turn R and pass the lake. **Turn L** immediately into a small park. Soon cross to the left-hand side of the river by the mill house. Cycle beside the Hogsmill, an interesting meander with several planked bridges to cross, and then under the railway bridge. **Turn L** up the short steep slope.

Now follow residential roads. **Turn R** along Eastcroft Road and **bear R** into Northcroft Road. **Bear L** into Plough Road and immediately cross over and **bear R** into Poole Road following the cycle lane.

Turn R into Heatherside Road and **L** into Scotts Farm Lane. **Turn L** at the T-junction into Ruxley Lane and cross over into a service road. Follow this road which **bears R** into Cox Lane. Cycle on past the Cox Lane Centre and into the narrow cycle path.

Turn L at the Hogsmill and follow the stream to the Chessington Road. **Turn L** and ride (or walk on the pavement) for about ⅓ mile. Cross near the Blue Chip Garage and look for a narrow opening on the right marked Horton Country Park.

Cycle along the path for ¼ mile and then **fork L**. Soon there is a T-junction of paths. **Turn R** and follow the marked cycle-way straight ahead through the park. This is idyllic cycling with a well-surfaced quiet path in a pastoral setting. In June the fields are ablaze with buttercups.

In 1¼ miles **turn L** at a T-junction and ride up the hill. **Turn R** opposite Primrose Cottage along a signed cycle track which passes a totem pole, and soon **bear R**. In 200 yards go through the opening in the fence and **turn L** into a lane. **Bear R** and **R** again to pass the entrance of West Park Hospital and into a bridleway signposted Christchurch Road.

Cross the busy road and ride onto Epsom Common. **Turn R** along the signed cycle track. Soon you pass Stew Pond where you may see Canada geese and other wildlife. Continue on the track up the slope and **bear L** at the top still following the signs. Ride around the common for 1¼ miles **bearing L** to keep on the main pathway. Where several paths meet **turn R** towards the Wells. Leave the Common and **turn L** into Wells Road. Cycle for ½ mile to the A24.

Cross into a grassy pathway and in ¼ mile **turn L** at a T-junction and cycle along the track. **Turn R** into Woodcote Side. At a T-junction **turn L** and ride in the cycle lane past Epsom Hospital. At the Ladas **turn R** into Chalk Lane, pushing your bike as this is one-way for 100 yards. Climb the hill and **bear R** onto the path beside the racecourse and back to the car park.

To extend your ride **turn R** by the Rubbing House, later linking with the cyclepath back to Tattenham Corner.

EPSOM

When cattle refused to drink the water from a spring in the early 17th century tests revealed that the water had a high level of magnesium sulphate. The water became famous for its medicinal qualities and wealthy people from London came to take the healing waters of Epsom's wells. Epsom Salts were renowned for helping to relieve indigestion.

EPSOM COMMON

This is a Site of Special Scientific Interest where there are large areas of developing

A family of goslings on Epsom Common

woodland and open areas are maintained to preserve the diverse flora. The Abbots of Chertsey constructed the two ponds in the 12th century. The smaller one is known as Stew Pond, which means fish pond, and in late spring it is worth visiting simply to see the Canada geese with their young. The larger is a wildlife reserve.

NONSUCH MANSION AND THE FORMER PALACE

The Mansion, built by Sir Jeffrey Wyattville and completed in 1806, stands on the site which surrounded Nonsuch Palace in the 16th century. It is now in Local Authority ownership and part is let to Sutton College of Liberal Arts for Adult Education. Henry VIII built the Tudor Palace of the original site, making it one of the most remarkable buildings of its time due to its magnificence, elegance and state of the art ornamental grounds. It was demolished in the 17th century but a great archaeological excavation was made in 1959 to unearth the foundations. The site is now marked only by three stone obelisks marking the length of the outer and inner courts.

4

Ripley, Pyrford and Wisley

14 miles

The River Wey towpath is a main feature of this route. Ride to Send Marsh, passing the lake and sailing club where you may be lucky and see glimpses of multi-coloured sails, enjoy the pastoral scenery around Send church and then ride to Cartbridge and the start of your route on the towing path. There are colourful, flowery narrow boats plying the river in the warmer weather. Experience the scene at Papercourt Lock where the weir rushes over three steps and later gaze at Pyrford Lock with its picturesque bridge. Cross the disused airfield at Wisley and spend some time in Ripley village.

Maps: OS Landranger 186 Aldershot and Guildford and 187 Dorking and Reigate (GR 040573).

Starting point: Car park at Newark New Bridge, near Ripley. Leave the M25 at junction 10 and join the A3 in the direction of Guildford. Make your way to the centre of Ripley and turn right into Newark Lane, signposted Pyrford. Pass the Seven Stars pub. At a warning sign for a humpback bridge prepare to turn left into the car park immediately before the bridge.

By train: West Byfleet is the nearest station at 2½ miles from the route.

Refreshments: There is the New Inn at Cartbridge and the Anchor at Pyrford Lock. RHS Wisley car park has a van selling sandwiches and drinks. More pubs are available in Ripley and Send Marsh.

The route: This follows quiet lanes, the River Wey towpath, a bridleway and some stretches of B road. It is relatively flat. The towpath offers beautiful scenery but is unsurfaced between Cartbridge and Walsham weir so expect your ride to be bumpy from time to time.

Turn R out of the car park along the B367 past the Seven Stars. In ⅓ mile **turn R** into Polesden Lane where you may see multi-coloured sails on the lake.

In ⅔ mile **turn R** at the grassy triangle in Send Marsh and **turn R** again to join the B368. Pass Aldertons and in ½ mile cross straight over at the traffic lights into Send Hill. Ride down to the crossroads and cross straight over to make a short detour to Send church which dates back to the 13th century. Even if the church is closed this lane offers a quiet ride flanked by fields where you can see a glimpse of Send Court, a beautiful old farmhouse.

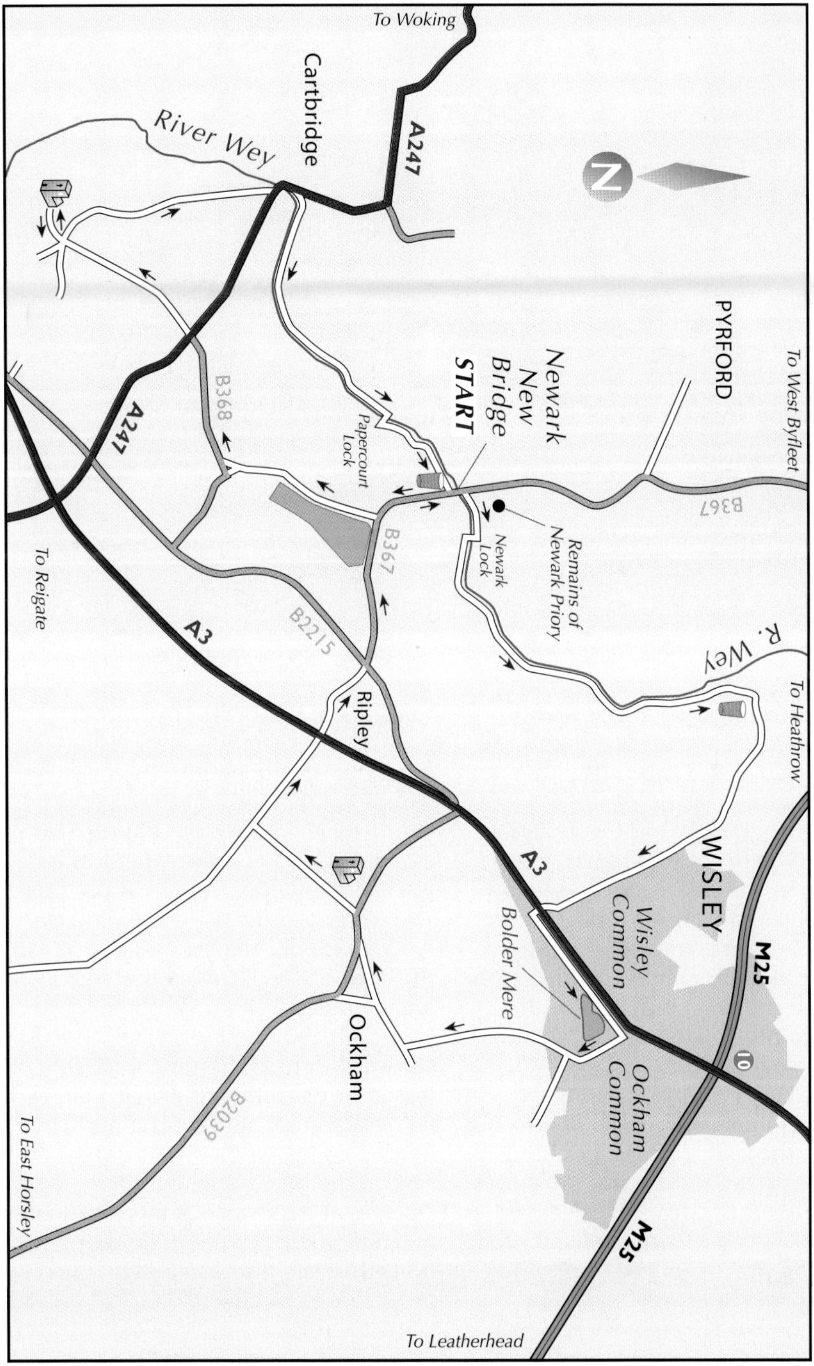

To Woking
Cartbridge
River Wey
A247
PYRFORD
To West Byfleet
Newark
New
Bridge
START
Papercourt
Lock
B368
A247
B367
Remains of
Newark Priory
Newark
Lock
B367
R. Wey
To Reigate
B2215
A3
Ripley
To Heathrow
WISLEY
Wisley
Common
A3
Bolder Mere
M25
Ockham
Ockham
Common
10
B2039
To East Horsley
M25
To Leatherhead

Papercourt Lock

Return to the crossroads and **turn L** along Vicarage Lane for just over a mile in the direction of Cartbridge.

Turn L onto the A247 at Cartbridge past the New Inn. Cross the bridge (keeping on the same side) and **turn L** immediately pushing your bike down the ramp to cross beneath the bridge and cycle along the River Wey towpath. It is a peaceful stretch of river with moored narrow boats and the chance of seeing some wildlife.

In just over a mile you reach Papercourt Lock and the weir. This is a beautiful place just to stand and stare. Cross over here to the other side of the river and wend your way on the right-hand bank of the river. You may need to push in places. At the road **turn L** over the bridge and then **R** to join the towpath again. (The car park is just here.)

Continue to follow the Wey for 2 miles. Cross the bridge at Newark Lock and cycle on the right of the river. Notice the remains of Newark Priory to your left. The priory was founded by Ruald de Calva and his wife for the Augustinian Order in the 12th century. The Order became large and powerful landowners but the Priory suffered with the dissolution of the monasteries after four centuries.

Cross a weir at Walsham Lock. Each season brings different delights along the path and in autumn the mist can be seen rising, with leaves brilliant against the river background. The path emerges at Pyrford Lock by the Anchor pub and you can see Pyrford Marina just across the humped bridge on the other side of the river.

From the Anchor go straight ahead

along Lock Lane for rather less than 2 miles. Passing through the village of Wisley the lane becomes Wisley Lane and you will soon pass the exit from the Royal Horticultural Society at Wisley Gardens. Continue to the entrance and **turn R** towards the gardens but do not go through the gates unless you are considering snacks from the van or looking around the gift shop.

Turn L along the path, signposted for the Guildford-bound bus stop, Elm Lane. This is a pedestrian path and easy shallow steps lead you over the A3 footbridge. Ride straight ahead to join the pedestrian/cycle path beside the A3 for just over ¾ mile. The traffic thunders towards you but you are safely separated from it. A stretch of water, peaceful Bolder Mere, comes into view on your right.

Turn R into Old Lane, a road bordered by woods. **Turn R** with care in about ½ mile at a sharp bend sign into a wide track. Almost immediately **fork L** and go round a barrier gate. For the next mile ride through woods, through the middle of a nature reserve, across the disused Wisley runway and straight on between the metal barriers to Bridge End Farm which has a dairy herd. The track turns to surfaced road and runs downhill to a T-junction.

Turn R into Ockham Lane. Very soon you will see the Hautboy restaurant to your left. **Fork R** and soon **turn R** onto the B2039 for a few yards then **turn L** into Guileshill Lane.

In about ¾ mile **turn R** at the crossroads into Rose Lane which leads into Ripley village. Having explored the village, cross to Newark Lane, signposted to Pyrford and the car park is on your left-hand side soon after the Seven Stars pub.

RIPLEY

This was a staging post in the 18th and 19th centuries on the route between London and Portsmouth and it was because of its importance that Ripley grew. In the 1890s the bicycle became very popular as a means of reaching the countryside and a ride to Ripley along the Portsmouth Road was a favourite trip from London. The Talbot Hotel and the Anchor were meeting places for cycling clubs. There are many interesting old buildings, some with gables and half-timbered. The green lies on the west side of the village.

WISLEY GARDENS

The Royal Horticultural Society gardens spread over 60 acres. There are extensive lakes, demonstration gardens and herbaceous borders. If you have time to spare at the end of your ride why not spend some time here. If you stop whilst on the route, find the refreshment van to the right of the car park and close to the buildings. There are a large gift shop and an extensive plant centre to browse around.

5

Pirbright, the Basingstoke Canal and Lightwater

20 miles

From the attractive village of Pirbright this route takes you past heathland and ranges to the Basingstoke Canal, a beautiful waterway where a short detour along the towpath offers a flight of 14 locks. Ride through Deepcut and over Chobham Ridges where army exercises take place, as much of this area is home to the British Army. Ride off-road into Lightwater Country Park to enjoy views to London from High Curley. Then travel along quiet country lanes towards Chobham, walk by the unusual ford and ride to Pennypot Lane, full of blossom in spring. The National Rifle Association at Bisley is on your return route.

Map: OS Landranger 186 Aldershot and Guildford (GR 946561).

Starting point: The car park at Pirbright. From the A322 make your way to Pirbright. The car park is on Avenue de Cagney by the village green and within sight of the Cricketers.

By train: Brookwood station is about a mile from the route.

Refreshments: Consider taking your own refreshments. There are two pubs at the start and the Basingstoke Canal Centre has a bright conservatory café which offers a variety of food and drinks. There is a Harvester at Frimley Green but no pubs on the route thereafter.

The route: There is a climb to Tunnel Hill but otherwise undulations are relatively few. Roads are not busy although there is some faster traffic on short stretches. The off-road riding is along the Basingstoke Canal and in Lightwater Park. Be prepared to push your bike up the 24 steps at Deepcut Bridge. Have patience with detailed directions from Windlesham Park. They keep you in the country away from busy roads.

From the car park **turn L** onto the A324 and immediately **R** along Church Lane past St Michael's church. In about ¾ mile **turn L** at the junction to pass Stoney Castle Ranges.

In a mile **bear L** past heathland for the climb up Tunnel Hill. Enjoy the downward sweep past Keogh Barracks. Soon there is a brown sign to the Canal Centre. **Turn R** just before the canal bridge and ride into the Centre. Browse through the information in the Centre and perhaps sample the pleasant café fare.

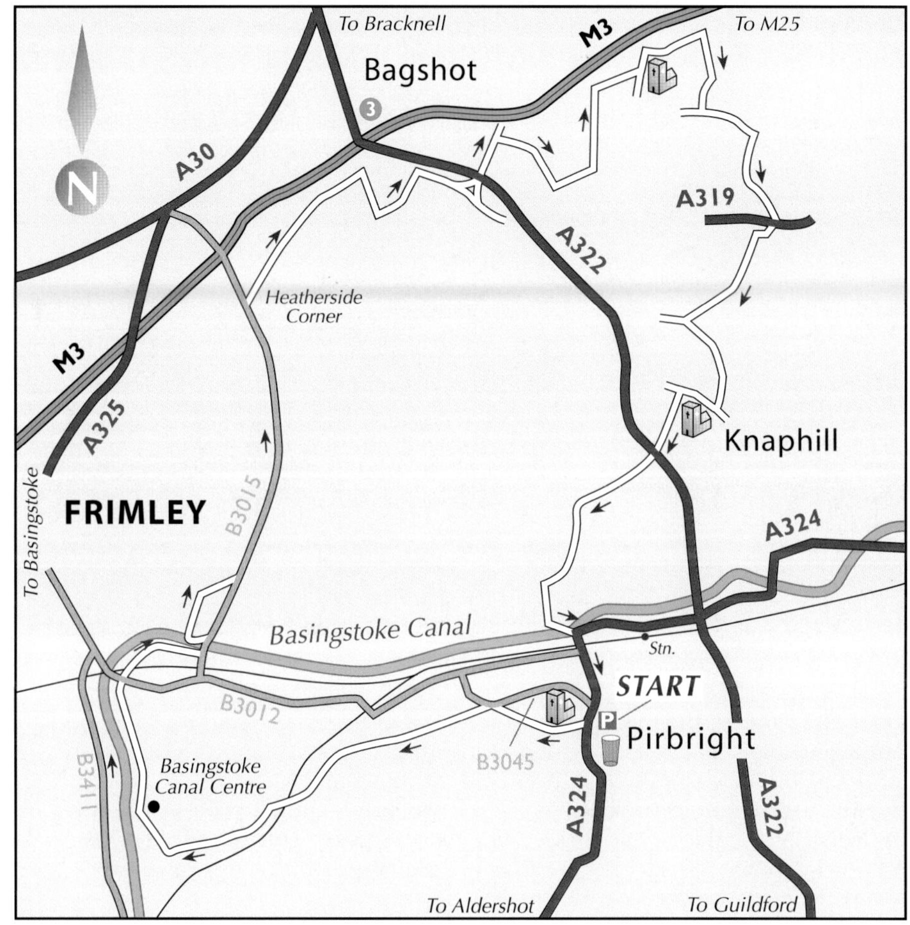

Pass the Centre and, pushing your bike, follow the towpath to the swing bridge. Cross over to the other bank, **turn R** and cycle along the canal towpath that is shared with pedestrians.

At the first bridge **bear L** and **turn R** onto the B3012 to cross the bridge. A Harvester pub is to your left. **Turn L** onto the towpath on the north bank of the canal. In ½ mile at Deepcut Bridge get off and push your bike up the steps to the road above. Here you can make a detour along the towpath to see a flight of 14 locks.

Returning from the locks, **turn R** onto the B3015, cross the canal and shortly **turn L** into Lake Road. Soon, opposite some bungalows, **turn R** into Bellew Road. Ride up the hill and follow the road round to the right.

Turn L at the junction onto the B3015 opposite the Royal Logistic Corps Museum. Ride for 2 miles to the roundabout at Heatherside Corner.

Take the second exit in the direction of Bagshot and dismount. Push your bike along the far left-hand footway for

Hammonds pond at Lightwater Country Park

about 200 yards to the point where it joins the road. There you can spot a concealed bridleway opposite. Cross over the road and into the narrow bridleway.

Follow the white markers delineating the bridleway for about ½ mile and look before crossing tracks which are used for vehicle testing. At a clearing keep straight ahead. Skirt to the right of a vehicle testing track and follow the narrow path ahead to High Curley at 129 metres high where there are views to London, Windsor Great Park and Guildford.

Turn around at High Curley and retrace a few steps. **Turn R** and go down the hill via a few steps (or the slope a few yards further on). **Turn R** at the base along a wide track. **Bear L** at marker post 6 and **R** at marker post 7 to join the nature trail to Hammonds Pond. This is a tranquil place where wildfowl nest. Keep ahead between the two ponds through the woods as far as a wire fence. **Turn R** to follow the bridleway.

Turn L into The Avenue and **R** at the T-junction and cycle for about ½ mile along this local road.

Turn L into All Saints Road in the direction of Windlesham and cycle over the A322. In less than ½ mile **turn R** into Hook Mill Lane wending past fields and woods for 1½ miles.

Turn R at the T-junction at Windlesham Park and ride to the next T-junction ½ mile away. **Turn L** signposted to Sunningdale.

Shortly **turn R** past the school into

Valley End Road. In ½ mile **turn R** signposted Sparrow Row. In ⅓ mile **bear R** into Woodcock Lane and pass an attractive thatched cottage.

Turn L at the T-junction and in ½ mile **R** into Ford Road and cycle to the unusual ford. Dismount and push your bike through the gate on the left and then **R** along the footpath beside the ford. Cross over the wooden bridge and **turn L**.

Turn R onto the A319 for a few yards and then **turn L** into attractive, winding Pennypot Lane for just over 1 mile. **Turn L** at Beldam Bridge towards Chobham.

In less than ¼ mile pass North Hill Nurseries and shortly **turn R** into the wide entrance to bridleway 176. **Fork R** near the top of the slope and follow the path as it runs between hedges across the golf course. **Bear R** at the bottom of the hill to Hill Place Farm.

Turn R into the lane and in ¼ mile **turn L** into Clews Lane. **Bear L** at the T-junction and cycle to the A322.

Cross the road at an offset crossing into Queen's Road. Cycle past Bisley Ranges. **Turn L** in about 1½ miles at a T-junction. In a short distance **turn L** again and ride over the Basingstoke Canal.

Turn R at the next junction to the traffic lights. Cycle under the railway bridge and in ½ mile you reach Pirbright Green and the car park.

LIGHTWATER COUNTRY PARK

This is a 143 acre park with a Heathland Visitor Centre for detailed information. Heathland is now highly valued for wildlife and offers feeding and breeding sites. There are many varieties of birds, wildfowl, deer, badgers and foxes. This park has high conservation value and has been designated a Site of Special Scientific Interest.

THE BASINGSTOKE CANAL

The canal extends from north Hampshire to the Thames. It is navigable and the towpath is open for 32 miles from the Greywell Tunnel which is a habitat for bats. The canal is a nature reserve, teeming with wildlife and its bridges and locks date back 200 years. It is worthwhile to take a detour along the towpath to see the start of the 14 locks between Pirbright and Deepcut which raise the canal by 100 ft.

THE CANAL VISITOR CENTRE, MYTCHETT

Browse in the canal exhibition at the Visitor Centre where you can experience the sights and sounds of Greywell Tunnel and see how barge skippers lived, learn about the restoration of the canal and about the wildlife habitats. There is an admission fee. Telephone: 01252 370073.

6

Great Bookham Common, Ockham and West Horsley

18 miles

This is a rural ride midst commuterland. Cycle on bridleways with views of the downs and along quiet lanes which weave over and under the M25. Ride across National Trust land at Great Bookham Common, an area of 452 acres on the dip slope of the North Downs. This is where the chalk of the North Downs meets London Clay resulting in peaceful lakes and wildlife. Cycle past Downside Common and The Cricketers, an atmospheric pub, and on to the outskirts of Cobham. Visit Chatley Heath Semaphore Tower, a relic of naval communication history, and see the attractive houses in Ockham Lane. Return via West Horsley using lanes and a tranquil farm road.

Map: OS Landranger 187 Dorking and Reigate (GR 130557).

Starting point: The car park on Great Bookham Common close by the station. From Leatherhead take the A246. Turn right along the High Street at Great Bookham and follow the road for a mile and the car park is on the right immediately before the station.

By train: Bookham station is at the start of the route.

Refreshments: The Plough near Cobham Park, the Swan at Hatchford, the Barley Mow at West Horsley and the Cricketers at Downside Common.

The route: There are gentle ascents and descents on quiet roads. The off-road riding is on Bookham Common, on a farm road and a short section is on the softer surface of Ockham Common. Lengthen this route by detouring to the village of Ripley. Shorten it to about 10 miles by looping homewards via Downside after visiting the semaphore tower.

From the car park cycle along the bumpy metalled lane across the common. Pass cottages on your far right. **Bear L** as the track divides and follow the path past still lakes to an area known as the 'Isle of Wight'. This is an open grassy area with a National Trust information board and Merritts Cottage is on your left. **Fork R** as the bridleways divide and ride to the edge of the common. **Bear L** onto Bookham Road and ride for nearly 2 miles. You cycle along a wonderfully peaceful lane between fields on the gently rising road and pass beneath the M25. Pass Downside Common, some attractive cottages and then the entrance to Cobham Park.

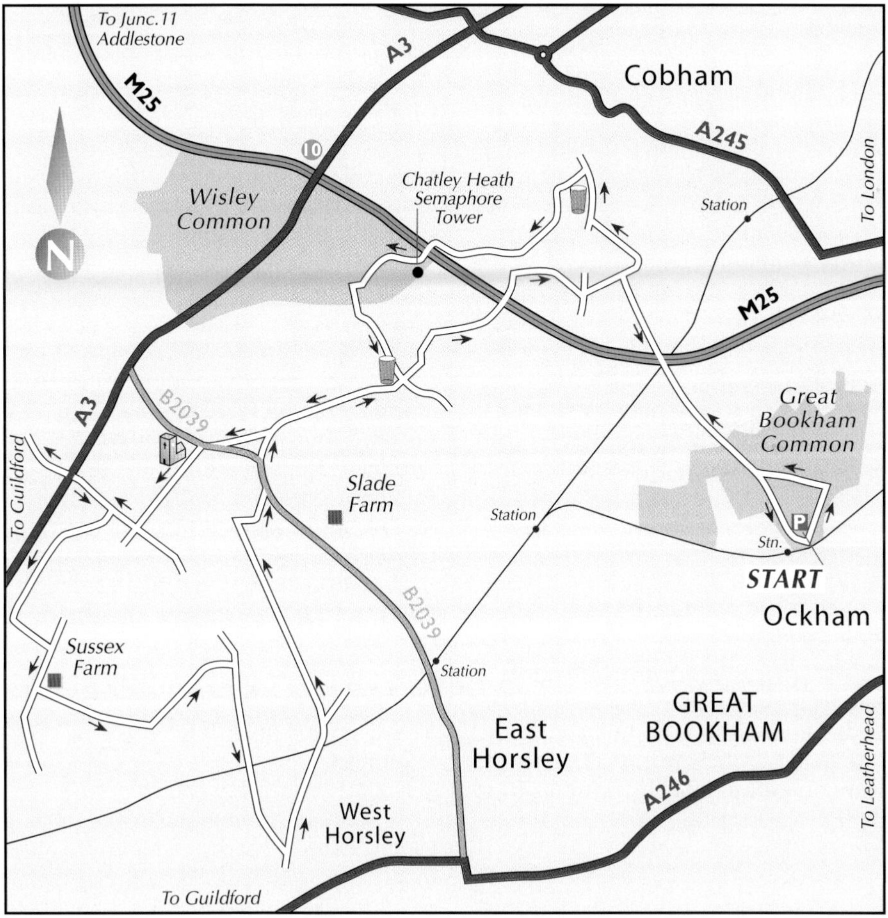

At the T-junction **turn R** in the direction of Cobham and in about ⅓ mile **turn L**, signposted to Hatchford, just past the gates of Logica. The Plough is soon on your left where you may feel that you cannot resist a relaxing break at a pub that claims to have the best burgers in Surrey!

Ride on from the pub and in about ½ mile **bear R** into Pointers Road and travel along this quiet and tree-shaded lane for ½ mile. **Turn L** along a metalled bridleway signposted to Chatley Heath Semaphore Tower and cross the M25. Traffic thunders beneath you. Climb the lane to the semaphore tower. Leave the tower and **turn R** down the bridleway which wends its way between rhododendrons and pines. The path widens as it is joined by other tracks. Just over ½ mile from the tower there is a barrier. **Turn L** and in less than ¼ mile go round another barrier into Old Lane.

Turn L and ride up the road to the Black Swan. **Turn R** into Ockham Lane and cycle for nearly a mile. As you ride down the hill there are attractive cottages and the Hautboy Restaurant. **Fork R** at the war memorial that commemorates the men of Ockham who served in each world war.

Turn R and then **L** along Guileshill Lane by the drive to All Saints church. Ockham Park is beyond the church but little remains of the original 17th-century building. There is now 2 miles of gentle riding around the lanes of rural Ripley. **Turn R** at the T-junction and cycle for about 200 yards.

You may wish to extend your ride by cycling straight ahead over the A3 into the village of Ripley. This return detour adds about 1¾ miles to your travels.

Turn L into Grove Heath Lane and pedal for over a mile as it becomes Gambles Lane and bends sharply to the left. Watch for glimpses of the North Downs. **Turn R** at a T-junction and cycle for about ⅓ mile past timbered Sussex Farm. **Turn L** immediately along a concreted bridleway past Holride Farm and enjoy the exhilaration of cycling for 1½ miles in traffic free rural countryside.

Turn R in the direction of West Horsley and ride for just over 1 mile passing under a railway bridge. **Turn L** into Pincott Lane soon after Dene Place Nursing Home on your right. Ride up the hill and past some attractive gardens. **Turn L** and in just over ½ mile ride under the railway bridge. Soon the Barley Mow pub is on your left.

Fork L shortly and ride for about 2 miles along Longreach, another quiet road that is edged by pasture-land. **Turn L** at the T-junction with Ockham Road and immediately **R** along Alms Heath. Retrace a mile of the route you rode earlier and cross straight over the crossroads to the Black Swan pub. Ride up and down the hill and cross high above the M25. In a few yards **turn R** into Chilbrook Road.

In ½ mile go straight over the crossroads and the Cricketers pub is on your left. If you are here when it is open it is a very attractive place to rest and enjoy views across the Common.

From the crossroads ride straight ahead to the edge of the common and **turn R** along Bookham Road. Retrace your outward journey for a mile back to Bookham Common and **turn R** along the main gravelled bridleway. At the 'Isle of Wight' **bear R** through the barrier by the information board and then **turn L** along the rough road. The car park is to your right at the end of the road.

ST MARY'S CHURCH, WEST HORSLEY

This is a 13th-century church on the A246 south-east of the route. The Pilgrim's Way is nearby and it is thought that the 13 ft high St Christopher wall painting was painted to bring them good fortune if they sighted him. It is claimed that the head of Sir Walter Raleigh was buried in St Nicholas' chapel by his son, Carew, who inherited the West Horsley Estate.

THE SEMAPHORE TOWER, CHATLEY HEATH

The tower, built in 1822, was one of a series of 13 semaphore stations between the Admiralty in Whitehall and the Royal Naval Dockyard in Portsmouth. Between 1796 and 1848 messages were sent by visual telegraphs from one tower to the next. By visiting the tower you can see

Chatley Heath semaphore tower

The Cricketers, Downside Common

some wonderful views, visit the exhibition and learn about the lives of its superintendents and their families. For opening times, telephone 01932 862762.

POLESDEN LACEY

This beautiful National Trust-owned property with its landscaped gardens is 2 miles to the south of Great Bookham and if you are still feeling energetic, a place to visit after your ride. There is a fine collection of furniture, paintings and porcelain and the grounds are a delight to walk around, with a rose garden, lawns with views to Ranmore Common and landscaped walks. The Queen Mother spent part of her honeymoon there.

7

Woking, the Basingstoke Canal and the River Wey

20 miles

This is for the most part a wander by waterways on towpaths. Join the Basingstoke Canal near Brookwood and follow the nature corridor to the junction with the Wey Navigation. You are likely to see fishermen, narrow boats and cascading weirs. Watch for the wildlife of the canal: swans taking flight, numerous species of dragonfly, water vole, heron and other wild life. You will also see the buildings of Woking and the M25 from a peaceful vantage point. Leave the towpath to visit the ruins of the Muslim Cemetery on the edge of Horsell Common, or if you are with children visit Burpham Court Farm Park and enjoy the rare breeds and Conservation Centre.

Maps: OS Landranger 186 Aldershot and Guildford and a tiny bit of 187 Dorking and Reigate (GR 987543).

Starting point: Whitmoor Common car park. From Guildford Town Centre take the A320 Woking road. Turn left into Burdenshott Road which is about ¼ mile past the Jacobswell roundabout. Drive for about ½ mile and the car park is on the left-hand side by the Jolly Farmer freehouse.

By train: Worplesdon, Woking or West Byfleet stations are close by the route.

Refreshments: Filippo's Café, St John's, serves deli food at tables near the canal; 1¼ miles further on cross over the canal bridge to Bridge Barn, a pub and restaurant. There are also the Anchor at Pyrford, Seven Stars at Newark and New Inn at Cartbridge.

The route: Towpath riding is usually easy, pleasant riding and is level. There is about 4½ miles of road riding but this is mostly quiet with only two ½ mile sections on busier roads. There is some walking required near Triggs Lock on a footpath.

Turn L out of the car park at Whitmoor Common. Keep cycling for ¾ mile and after a downhill slope **bear L** into Smart's Heath where the road bends sharply right. At a T-junction **turn L** onto the B380 for ½ mile and then **turn R** signposted to Brookwood.

Ride for 1½ miles past paddocks, a majestic row of pines and under the railway. Cross the A324 into a track to the left of the bridge and immediately

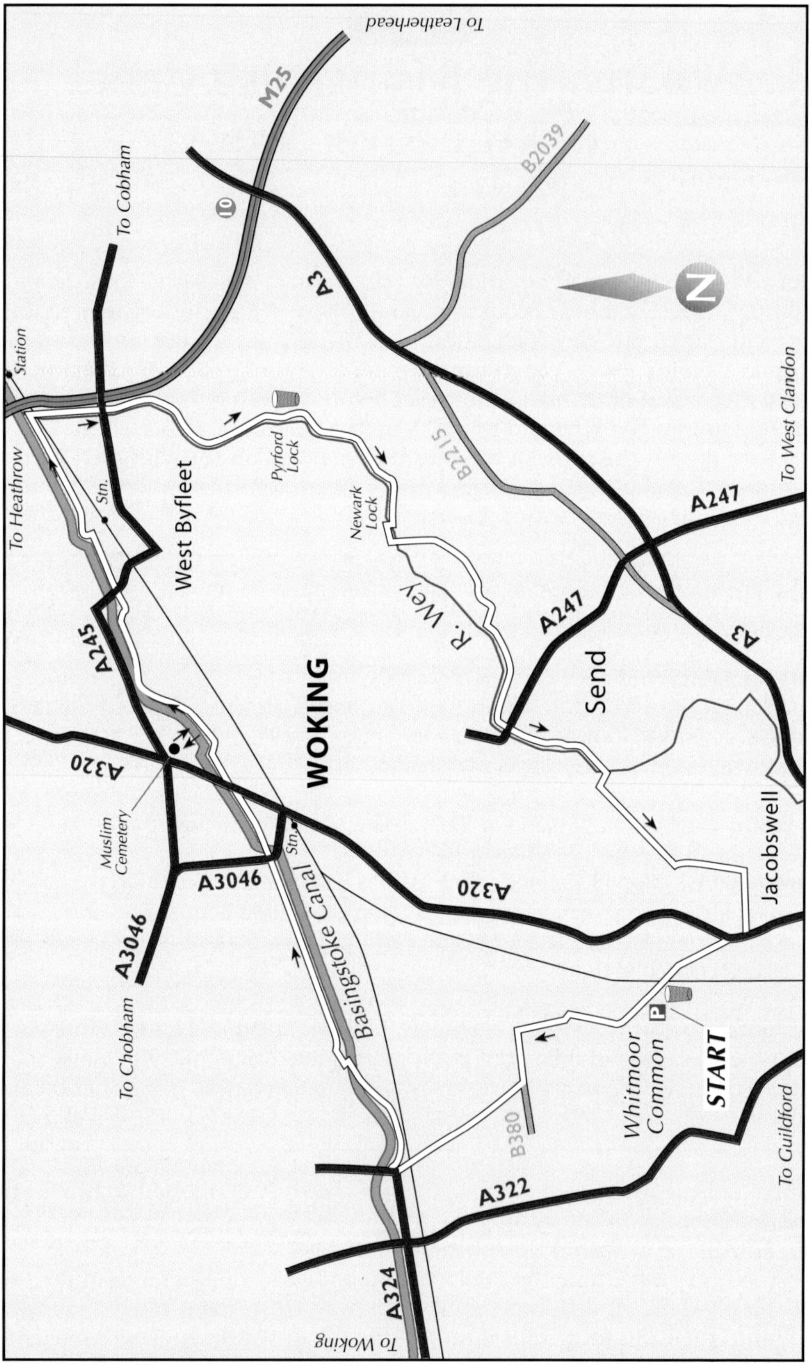

To Leatherhead
M25
B2039
To Cobham
10
A3
N
Station
To Heathrow
Stn.
West Byfleet
Pyrford Lock
Newark Lock
B2215
To West Clandon
A247
A247
R. Wey
A3
Send
A245
WOKING
A320
Muslim Cemetery
Stn.
A3046
A3046
A320
Jacobswell
Basingstoke Canal
To Chobham
P
START
Whitmoor Common
B380
To Guildford
A322
A324
To Woking

Pyrford Lock

turn R towards the Basingstoke Canal. **Turn R** again along the towpath in the direction of St John's.

At St John's cross to the north bank of the canal. There are a series of descents by five locks which are fun to ride but remember to give way to pedestrians. In 1¼ miles you can use the bridge to reach Bridge Barn Restaurant on the far bank and return to the route. Cycle on along the towpath for ¾ mile to Woking and cross the A3046.

Cross over to the south side of the canal and ride for 1 mile to the far side of a bridge opposite a large office block, Britannia Wharf. Make a detour here to the Muslim Cemetery. Push your bike up to the road, over the bridge and through the car park by the offices. In about 200 yards you will see the ruins of the cemetery on your right.

Return to the towpath and ride for 2 miles passing Sheerwater and six Woodham Locks. This is a ride along the peaceful canal bank past gardens and woodland until you reach an unexpected spaghetti junction ahead.

Cross the bridge over the Wey Navigation and **turn R** along the towpath riding under the Waterloo to Woking railway line. The M25 runs alongside. In ½ mile **turn L** at a road and then **bear R** to follow a narrow path back to the towpath.

As you approach Pyrford Lock the Anchor pub is on your left. The area is beautiful and a rest here should offer a peaceful view of narrow boats passing by as they make their way under the

The Muslim Cemetery, Woking

bridge to the lock. Opposite is Pyrford Marina.

Ride on along the towpath to Newark Lane for about 2 miles, crossing the weir at Walsham Lock. The last mile is not surfaced but is easily rideable in normal conditions.

Cross to the far bank at Newark Lock. **Turn L** at the road and cycle over the bridge. The Seven Stars pub is on your right in about ¼ mile.

Turn R here into Papercourt Lane where there are some long views across the meadows towards the river. In ¾ mile there is a large building on your right called Tannery House. **Turn R** into a narrow pathway immediately before the building. Ride over the River Wey and **turn L** along the towpath.

Cartbridge is about 1 mile along the path. Push your bike under the bridge, up the ramp and cross the river to the New Inn. Cycle along the east side of the river and enjoy the easy ride and the picturesque scenes along the ½ mile to Worsfold Gates where there is a weir. Triggs Lock is ¾ mile further across two bridges and over a grassy stretch where you may need to get off and push. This is a very attractive lock viewed from either bank.

Cross to the other side of the river by pushing your bike up and down the three steep steps on either side of the lock. **Bear R** on the footpath, pushing your bike for ½ mile or so. Go between the stiles and **turn L** along Runtleywood. Then **bear L** into Robin Hood Lane and **L** into Sutton Green Road where you will soon pass the Fox and Hounds pub. Ride up Blanchard Hill to Jacobswell.

Turn R at the T-junction (unless you are visiting Burpham Court Farm Park which is ½ mile to your left). At the A320 cross the busy road with care and **turn R**. On your left you pass Willow Grange, home of the Bishops of Guildford. Shortly **turn L** into Burdenshott Road and ride for just over ½ mile back to Whitmoor Common.

THE RIVER WEY AND THE WEY NAVIGATION

The Wey Navigation links Guildford to Weybridge and the Thames in a 15½ mile navigable waterway. One of the first rivers to be made navigable, it was opened to barge traffic in 1653. In 1764 the Godalming Navigation was also opened enabling barges to travel even further up river. Now owned by the National Trust there is a centre at Dapdune Wharf, Guildford, where you can see a restored Wey barge and an exhibition telling the story of the waterway, the people who lived and worked on it and the barges built there. Telephone 01483 561389 for information regarding Dapdune Wharf.

THE MUSLIM CEMETERY, WOKING

Amidst the pines are the shadowy ruins of the Muslim Cemetery, built in 1915 for Indian soldiers killed during the First World War. The graves have been removed but the domed archway with its fronds of ivy and brick walls remain, surrounding a tranquil quadrangle. Horsell Common Preservation Society are raising funds to restore the cemetery.

BURPHAM COURT FARM PARK

Burpham Court Farm Park lies just off the return route. It is open March to October, and a tearoom is open at weekends. Telephone: 01483 576089.

8

West Humble, Leatherhead, Epsom Downs and Headley

19 miles

Ride through West Humble to the bridleways of Norbury Park and visit Bocketts Farm, a working family farm where you can enjoy the tearoom in the 18th century barn. More bridleways lead close to the centre of Leatherhead across the River Mole. Then climb to Epsom Downs where you see the Grandstand silhouetted against the skyline and may see racehorses exercise in the mornings; try the route on Derby Day and share the exhilarating atmosphere of the races. Go and browse at a working forge and enjoy a long cruise downhill along Lodgebottom Road. If you have energy to spare, detour up the steep Zig Zag Road to Box Hill, gaze at the long views over Dorking to the South Downs and visit the National Trust shop and kiosk.

Map: OS Landranger 187 Dorking and Reigate (GR 172522).

Starting point: The second car park on the left after the Burford Bridge Hotel. Take the A24 from Leatherhead in the direction of Dorking. At the Mickleham/Boxhill roundabout take the first exit.

By train: Boxhill and Westhumble station is on the route. Bike hire is available at Sarah's Cycle Hire, Boxhill station, telephone: 01306 886944.

Refreshments: Boxhill station and Bocketts Farm Café, Norbury Park provide a variety of snacks. Pubs include the Tattenham Corner, the Derby Arms and the Rubbing House on Epsom Downs.

The route: Some ideal quiet lanes and on bridleways with short stretches on busier roads. There are some ups and downs but only one short sharp hill to Norbury Park. There are some stony tracks in Norbury Park.

Turn L out of the car park. Pass the Burford Bridge Hotel and **turn L** onto the pedestrian/cycle path beside the A24. In a few yards at the subway sign push your bike under the road. **Turn L** up the slope on the far side. **Turn R** in a few yards towards Westhumble past the Stepping Stones pub.

If open, try Sarah's at the station for a tantalising Cornish cake. Continue over the railway bridge and **turn R** in front of the arch into Crabtree Lane. The arch is in memory of Fanny Burney, an 18th century novelist and diarist who lived in Westhumble. Climb the steep hill for nearly a mile passing the car parks. Soon there are

wide views and you can see the spire of Ranmore church. Near the end of the metalled lane **turn R** along the bridleway opposite Crabtree Cottages. Bocketts Farm is 2 miles away through Norbury Park.

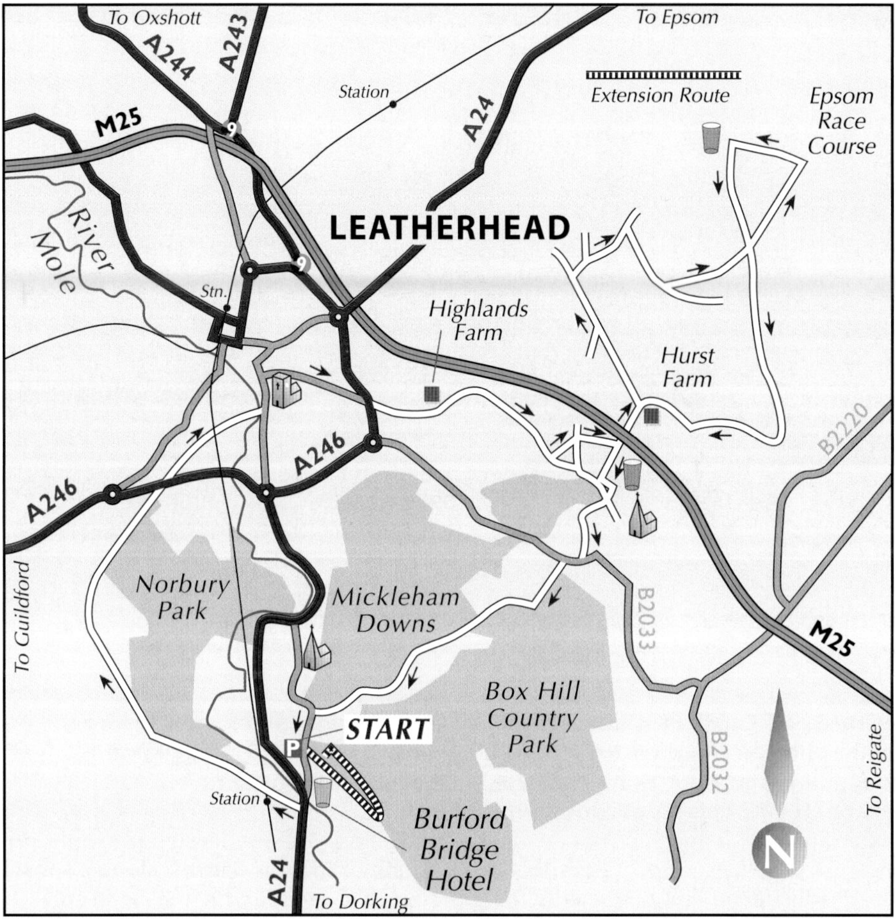

The path descends and then diverges by an open grassy triangle. **Fork R** and keep ahead to Bocketts Farm. You pass Roaring House Farm on your left and later cross into a narrow bridleway which winds its way past Bocketts Farm. There is a permissive footpath into the farm. Enjoy the tearoom in the barn or sit outside under an umbrella.

Return to the track (**turn R** from the farm) and ride for a few yards to the Leatherhead bypass. Cross the busy road and join the bridleway to Hawk's Hill. At a signpost, **fork R** in the direction of Gimcrack Hill and walk or ride down to the railway bridge. Soon you ride over the River Mole, a particularly scenic spot.

At the junction with the B2450 **turn L** for a short distance in the direction of

Box Hill is a popular viewpoint and picnic spot

Leatherhead. In about ¼ mile **turn R** by the church onto the B2033. **Fork L** at a mini-roundabout along Headley Road to the A24. Cross over using the bollard to your left.

On Headley Road climb gradually for 1½ miles and just past Headley Court **turn L** down Lea Green Lane. At the T-junction cross over and into the driveway opposite. In a few yards **bear L** through the gate onto the public byway through fields. In ⅓ mile **turn L** onto Walton Road and ride for nearly a mile.

Turn R at the T-junction into Headley Road where there are good views towards Leatherhead. In ⅓ mile **turn R** into busy Downs Road and enjoy the fast downhill sweep. In ½ mile **turn R** into the garage (for safety reasons) and turn round, retrace a few yards and **turn L** on the bridleway towards Langley Bottom Farm.

Ride along the bridleway for ½ mile passing the farm. **Turn L** along a short narrow footpath which leads steeply upwards to the Downs. (This is by a noticeboard but if you miss it the next two paths lead up to the same place.) Cross the gallop and ride along the metalled road ahead. It narrows and bends to the left. **Turn R** at the cross-tracks by the cottage. On for a mile to Tattenham Corner with the thrill of the grandstand and the racecourse laid before you. You have three pubs to choose from on the Downs.

Turn L along the B290 taking the cycle lane in the direction of the grandstand. At the roundabout take the second exit

(the one after the Banqueting Hall). **Turn L** off the road at the pedestrian lights into the path beside the racetrack. In a few yards **bear L** to cross the racecourse by the Rubbing House.

Cycle for 2 miles following the way marked as a pedestrian-cycle path. The surface and width change dramatically as it crosses the racecourse, crossing-path and gallops and descends over Walton Downs into Ebbisham Lane. Keep straight ahead whatever the terrain, though you will have to cycle over coconut matting! There are wide views and the spire of Headley church can be seen to the south.

Turn R at the junction into Hurst Road. At the junction with Walton Road **turn L**, still Hurst Road, and ride beneath the M25. At the T-junction there is a working forge that makes an interesting visit.

From Hurst Lane **turn L** up the hill and shortly **R** into Slough Lane, a delightful lane with pretty cottages. **Turn R** at the T-junction onto the B2033. In 200 yards **turn L** along Lodgebottom Road for 2 miles of wonderful downhill riding. At the T-junction **turn L** in the direction of Dorking and the car park is less than ½ mile on your right.

THE FORGE AT HEADLEY

There are three businesses in one, a farrier, a gift shop and a fabrication shop. You can watch the farrier making horse-shoes, see wrought-iron goods for sale and wander in the gift shop where there are candles and novelties. About 50% of the items for sale are made by the owners. Telephone: 01372 386417.

EPSOM DOWNS

Horse racing took place on Epsom Downs in the 17th century but it was in the 18th century that the Earl of Derby and Sir Charles Bunbury introduced the Oaks stakes for fillies and the Derby for colts. The Derby was so called because Sir Charles lost the toss, otherwise it would have been known as the Bunbury. The Derby takes place in June each year and there is quite a carnival atmosphere with a fair which also takes place on the Downs.

9

Leigh, Betchworth and Brockham

14 miles

This route threads its way through some of Surrey's most picturesque villages and takes you along delightful country roads. There are views to Box Hill on the North Downs and glimpses of the meandering River Mole. You may park on National Trust land at tranquil Fourwents Pond, ride to Leigh (pronounced Lye) where you see the church of St Barnabas dating back to the 15th century and the Priests' House on the village green. Your route winds by some beautiful old manor houses and you may be fortunate and see herds of deer through the iron gates at Wonham. Betchworth with its forge and Church of St Michael and the picture book village of Brockham are places to stop and wander or simply to soak up the atmosphere from a village seat.

Map: OS Landranger 187 Dorking and Reigate (GR 184455).

Starting point: Fourwents Pond. This is in Blackbrook Road on the eastern edge of Holmwood Common. Drive south from Dorking on the A24 for 2 miles. Turn left into Mill Lane, signposted Leigh and turn left again at the T-junction with Blackbrook Road. The free car park is a few yards on your left.

By train: Dorking and Deepdene stations are 1 mile from the route.

Refreshments: Choose between the Plough at Leigh, the Dolphin at Betchworth, the Duke's Head and the Royal Oak at Brockham. You will see other pubs on the homeward stretch.

The route: There are many quiet lanes and some gentle undulations. On the off-road section near Ewood there may be surface mud in prolonged wet weather. To avoid this section, begin by turning R out of the car park towards Newdigate. In 2 miles turn L at the T-junction in the direction of Charlwood. In 1 mile turn L into Shellwood Road immediately after the Surrey Oaks pub. Keep pedalling for 1½ miles. This adds about 1½ miles to the total mileage. Then continue at paragraph three below.

Turn R as you leave Fourwents car park. In a few yards **turn L** at the cross-lanes into Lodge Lane. **Turn R** at the end of the lane in front of the gateway to Lodge Farm into a concreted bridleway and ride under the railway bridge. This is the railway line that runs between Horsham and Dorking. Follow the concreted way with views towards the North Downs until you reach a cattle grid at a T-junction.

Turn R along the track and soon **fork R** as it divides. In less than ¾ mile you

reach some attractive cottages and Ewood Old Farm House. In ½ mile **bear R** at the post-box and in a few yards **turn L** along a narrow bridleway just past bungalows on your right. Join a wider driveway which leads to a T-junction by Bracken House. **Turn L** into Shellwood Road and keep pedalling for over a mile.

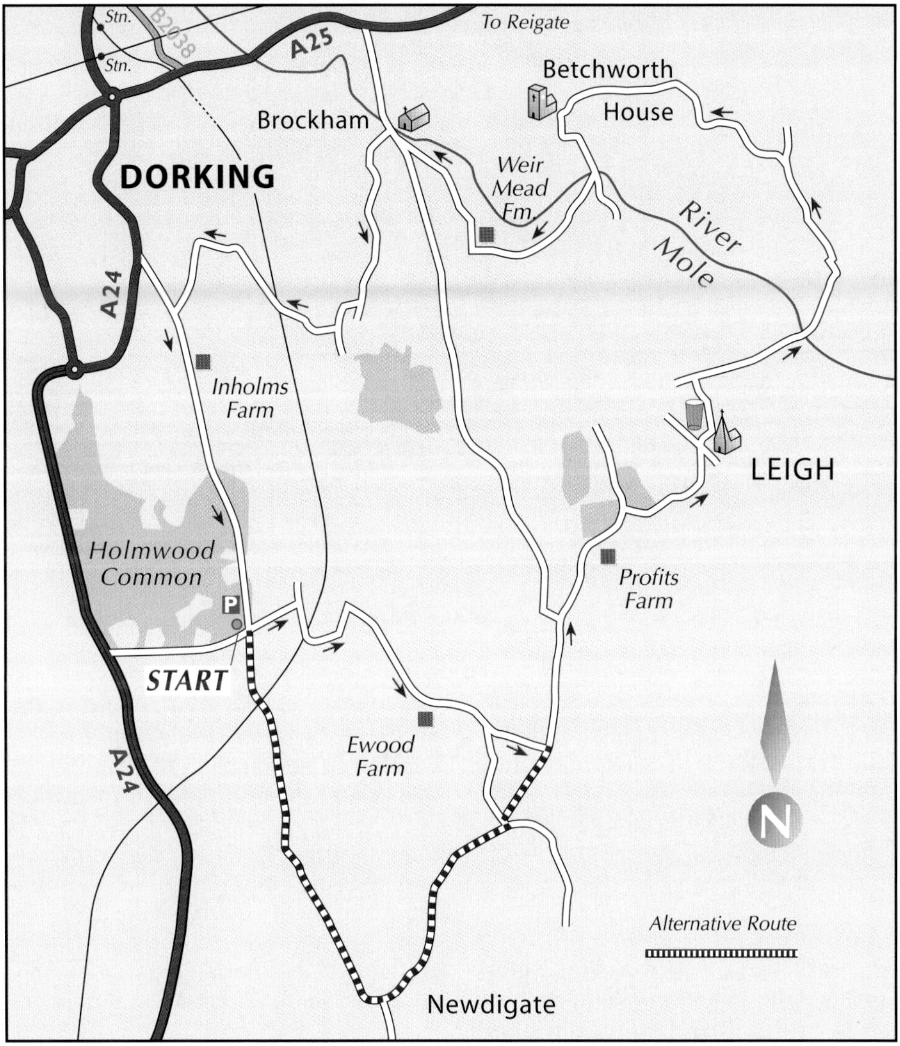

(The alternative road route joins here.) On the way you see views to the North Downs. Cross a narrow bridge and go past the end of Shellwood Road on your left. Ride up an incline past woods, fields and paddocks. **Turn R** into Clayhill Road, a winding lane leading past fields in the direction of Leigh.

At Leigh enjoy the picture of the

Deer at Wonham Manor, near Betchworth

village green with its church and to the right the fascinating terrace of irregular buildings known as the Priests' House. At the crossroads cycle straight ahead past the Plough and St Bartholomew's church and on past Leigh Place.

Turn R at the T-junction into Flanchford Road. Ride for about a mile past Bury Hill Prep School and over a narrow bridge. **Turn L** in the direction of Betchworth for just over ½ mile. The road winds past two manor houses. Pull into the gateway just past Stepstile Manor for views towards Box Hill. If you are fortunate you may see farm animals or even a llama or two.

Turn L into Trumpet's Hill Road which runs steeply downhill and is signposted Betchworth. **Bear L** past attractive houses. Soon on your right is Wonham Mill, a 19th-century water mill, then watch for the iron gates of Wonham Manor and the deer herds in the park.

The inviting seat outside the Dolphin at Betchworth may entice you to stop for refreshment. The old village forge is opposite. You can walk through the churchyard and out by the gate to see attractive timbered cottages.

Turn L at the T-junction signposted to Leigh. Ride for ½ mile across the narrow bridge over the River Mole and up the hill to **turn R** in the direction of Brockham. In less than a mile **turn R** into Wheeler's Lane opposite the recycling centre. **Turn R** at Christ Church in Brockham. There is a village shop on your left and two pubs across the green. **Turn L** into School Lane just past the old pump and ride past fields. **Turn R**

after 1 mile by Bushbury Farm into Parkpale Lane. In less than ¼ mile **turn R** again into narrow Tilehurst Lane and then ride on under the railway bridge. Cycle or push your bike up a shaded hill to a T-junction and **turn L** signposted to Holmwood.

Turn L at the T-junction into Blackbrook Road. This is the homeward stretch with some inclines for the last 1½ miles to Fourwents Pond which is on your right.

LEIGH

Leigh, like several other villages in the neighbourhood, is an old iron village. In the 16th century metal was extracted from ironstone and charcoal from local woodland was used to smelt the iron. Some of the power for the mill would have been provided by a small tributary of the Wey which flows through the village. The church has an interesting 3 ft high brass of John Arderne, and his family. He was High Sheriff of Surrey in 1432 and lived at Leigh Place which you pass after the church.

BROCKHAM

Brockham's name comes from the badgers to be found on the banks of the River Mole. It is a particularly attractive village and is much photographed. Christ Church is 13th-century in style but is actually Victorian and was built where there once was a duck pond. The church, two pubs and cottages line the green with the beautiful background of Box Hill. On a sunny day you can sit outside either the Duke's Head or the Royal Oak by the green and just enjoy the remarkable village. Leave the route for a moment and stroll over the River Mole on the old pedestrian bridge.

The village green, Brockham

10

Around the Hog's Back

22 miles

A lovely ride along the southern slopes of the Hog's Back and through the attractive villages of Compton, Puttenham and Seale. Travel a section of the Pilgrims' Way, visit Watts Gallery and Manor Farm Craft Centre and return north of the Hog's Back. Then ride along the River Wey towpath into Guildford, park your bike and explore the town on foot. This route is full of interest and nearly all away from busy traffic.

Map: OS Landranger 186 Aldershot and Guildford (GR 003484).

Starting point: The Chantries, Guildford. Take the A281 Horsham Road from Guildford and after 1 mile, opposite Shalford Park, turn left into Pilgrims' Way. Turn right in ¼ mile into the North Downs Way track. The car park is on your left.

By train: Wanborough and at Guildford where the River Wey towpath is close by.

Refreshments: Try the Harrow at Compton, the Good Intent at Puttenham village, the White Hart at Wood Street, or the Jolly Farmer at Guildford by the river. Watts Gallery, Compton has a café. Manor Farm Craft Centre has a tea-room and delicious cakes.

The route: Quite level. There is ½ mile on the busy B3000 but otherwise it is a quiet route. Be prepared to walk along two footpaths. The River Wey towpath is narrow on entering Guildford.

Turn L down the Pilgrims' Way to the A281. Cross at the bollard to Shalford Park. **Turn L** onto the cycle path for 1 mile following the cycle signs in the direction of Godalming.

Ride straight on by the Thames Water Treatment Offices and **bear R** at the top of the slope. Cross the railway and ride along the narrow path across the common. **Bear R** past the cottages to the A248, the Peasmarsh to Shalford road. The Parrot pub is opposite.

Turn R over the narrow bridge to join the pedestrian/cycle path on your right for ½ mile. **Turn L** into Oakdene Road. At the T-junction avoid the busy A3100 and cross into the gravelled drive opposite. Shortly **bear L**, pushing your bike for ⅓ mile along a grassy footpath and then through peaceful woodland.

Cross the B3000 and cycle into Summers Road past Broadwater School. In ¾ mile **turn R** across Farncombe railway crossing and cycle along Green

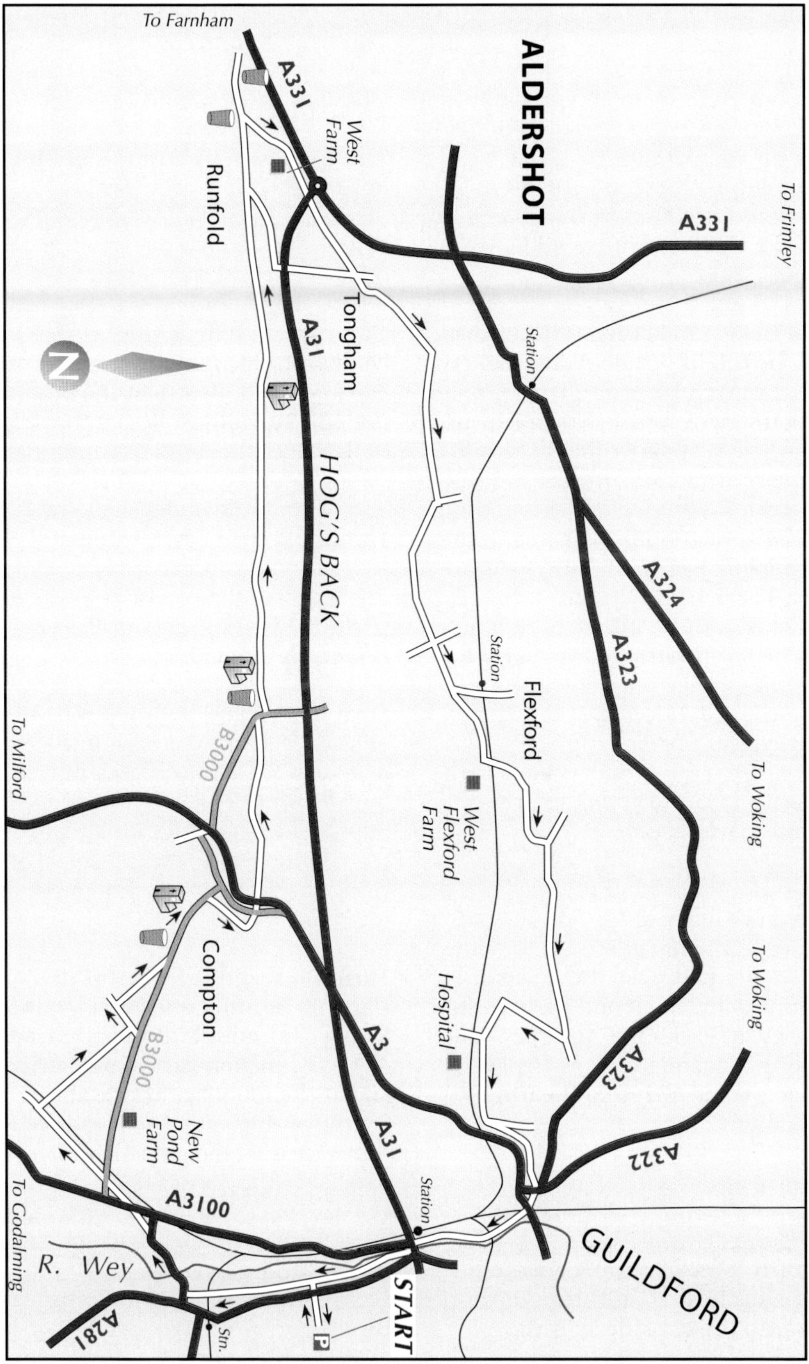

To Farnham
ALDERSHOT
To Frimley
A331
A331
West Farm
Runfold
Tongham
A31
Station
HOG'S BACK
A324
A323
Station
Flexford
To Woking
West Flexford Farm
B3000
To Milford
Compton
Hospital
To Woking
A3
A323
B3000
New Pond Farm
A31
A322
A3100
Station
To Godalming
R. Wey
GUILDFORD
A281
Stn.
START
P

Lane to the T-junction.

Turn L into Binscombe Lane and soon **R** into the Avenue. In about ¼ mile at Tythe Barn **bear L** and push your bike along the footpath to Compton (ignoring the bridleway). **Turn L** in Compton onto the busy B3000 and watch for the interesting Old Barn Antiques shop.

In less than ½ mile **turn R** into Down Lane. **Turn L** in ¼ mile (Watts Gallery is a few yards further on). For 1½ miles follow the signs for the North Downs Way as you ride under the A3, passing some very attractive cottages and a golf club. **Turn R** onto the B3000 opposite the Jolly Farmer pub. Soon **turn L** into Puttenham village past Puttenham Priory. The cottages are built of chalk and sandstone, as Puttenham lies on a line which separates the two. At the end of the village is a long downhill before you climb to Seale church and the delightful Manor Farm Craft Centre. The farm buildings have been converted into a tearoom, craft shop and music workroom.

Turn L along the Pilgrims' Way in the direction of Runfold for 1¼ miles. **Turn L** at the T-junction and then **R** by the Jolly Farmer pub. Take the 2nd exit at the mini-roundabout and perhaps stop to browse at Packhorse Antiques. Ride on along the lane to follow the cycle path across the A31, soon **bearing R** into Grange Road.

In ½ mile you reach Tongham crossroads. **Turn L** and watch for a small grassed area with seats on your left. **Turn R** into a narrow gravelled path opposite. In ¼ mile turn down the bank onto the old railway track.

Turn R in ½ mile between two barriers. This path becomes Ash Green Road West, crosses White Lane and becomes a bridleway for ½ mile.

At a T-junction by Pound Farm **turn R** onto a lane for ¼ mile passing Rickwood Farm. Follow the public byway signs onto a track and ride for ¾ mile to Christmas Pie crossroads.

Cross over and in ¼ mile, as the road bends left, ride straight ahead along Flexford Road. **Bear L** at the bottom of the hill. **Turn R** just before the railway bridge along the bridleway past fields.

Turn L and ride under the railway. For 1 mile follow the path through Cleygate Copse (**bear R** where the path divides) over the common to the haven of the White Hart pub, bedecked with flowers in summer.

Turn R and cycle round Wood Street village green and **R** again in the direction of Guildford. In a mile, at the lowest point before a small bridge and built up area, **turn R** into a track over the common. Go round the gate and along the footpath, pushing your bike for ⅓ mile.

Turn L through the barrier into Hartshill, **R** into Cabell Road, **L** into Stoneybank and **R** into Pond Meadow. At the T-junction **turn L** past shops and at the roundabout ride ahead into Southway. Just after the parade of shops **turn R** along a path which runs parallel to the A3 to Buckingham Road.

Turn R into Western Road and cross the footbridge over the A322 into Caxton Gardens. At Woodbridge Hill **turn R** and at the Wooden Bridge pub push your bike over the A3 footbridge.

The Packhorse Antiques Centre, Runfold

The ramp is to the left. Follow the cyclepath under the railway bridge and **turn R** into Woodbridge Meadows.

Where the railway crosses the road **bear L** across the grass to join the narrow Wey towpath into central Guildford. Cycle under two bridges and at Town Bridge continue past St Nicholas' church into Millmead.

Bear L in front of the Council Offices and push your bike over the pedestrian bridge. **Turn R** before attractive Millmead Lock and cycle for ¼ mile along the towpath past the Jolly Farmer pub to the footbridge over the river. Push your bike up the steps and over the bridge. **Turn R** to the Guildford Rowing Club boat house. Here you join a cycle path.

In about ¼ mile, just beyond the Shalford Pavilion, **turn L**, cross the A281 and retrace the route up the Pilgrims' Way. **Turn R** in ¼ mile along the North Downs Way track to the car park.

GUILDFORD

Guildford, which grew up around the river valley of the Wey, is a gap town in the North Downs. You can walk up the attractive cobbled High Street to explore its historic sights, shops and cafés. See the castle ruins, Abbotts Hospital where the almshouses are arranged around an internal courtyard, and the Tudor Guildhall with the often photographed clock. Tourist Information is available at Tunsgate, halfway up the High Street on the right.

The River Wey above Millmead Lock

WATTS GALLERY, COMPTON

George Frederick Watts was a Victorian portrait painter and sculptor. There is a purpose-built gallery where you can browse round the paintings and downstairs are some examples of his powerful sculpture. There is a restaurant on the site. Telephone: 01483 810235.

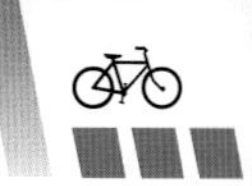

11

Shere Heath, Albury, Wonersh and Thorncombe Street

18 miles

South-east of Guildford and the North Downs lies a large area of heath and woodland, most of which is designated as an Area of Outstanding Natural beauty. This ride takes you through the villages of Albury, Chilworth, Blackheath, Wonersh and Bramley, continuing to the ruins of a Roman temple at Farley Heath, one of the oldest of Surrey's historic sites. There is some outstandingly beautiful countryside in the folds of the hills and along the Tillingbourne valley. Glance upwards to the chimneys of Albury, notice the timbered cottages in Wonersh and spot the unusual signpost at Blackheath.

Maps: OS Landranger 186 Aldershot and Guildford and 187 Dorking and Reigate (GR 061466).

Starting point: The car park at Albury Heath. Take the A25 and turn into the A248 west of Shere in the direction of Albury. In about ½ mile turn left at the sharp bend to pass Albury Park. In just over a mile there is a car park on your left before the road dips to the railway.

By train: Chilworth station is on the route.

Refreshments: The Drummond Arms, Albury; the Red Lion, Shamley Green, open all day; and the William IV at Albury. This is a lovely 16th-century pub with a stone floor and beams. All food is home cooked. There are other pubs sprinkled along the route in all the villages.

The route: This has some ups and downs and the climb to Farley Heath is followed by a good run down to Farley Green. There is some main road riding near the start in a 30 mile an hour limit. You can push your bike for a few yards on the pavement where you join the A281. Most of the route is quiet lanes and some off-road bridleway. To shorten the route: Turn left along the Wey South Path in Bramley just before St Catherine's School. In about 1¼ miles turn left sharply just past the Beaver yard and a planked bridge. This shortens the route by about 4 miles.

Turn R out of the car park. Ride down the hill in the direction of Albury. **Turn L** onto the A248 at the T-junction at the bottom of the hill. Cycle through the village of Albury with its tall chimneys and the Drummond Arms pub and follow the road for 1½ miles as it passes Lockner Farm on your right where there are good views up to St Martha's church perched on the hill.

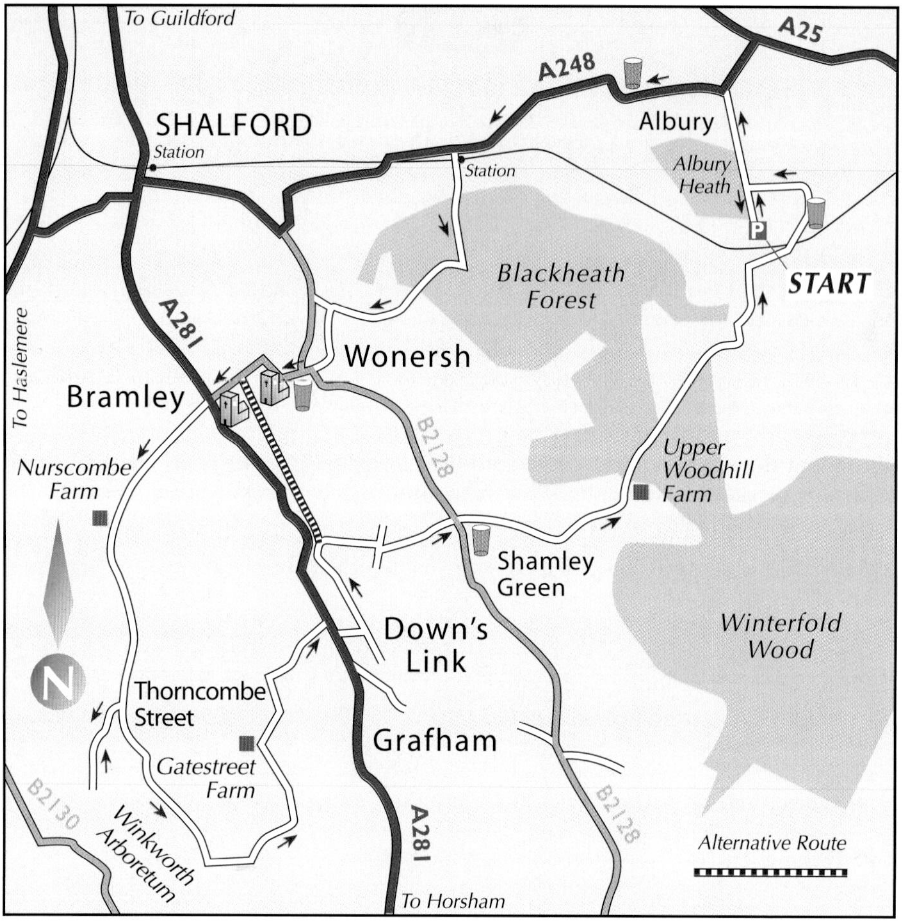

Turn L over the railway crossing at Chilworth station, and cycle up Sample Oak Lane in the direction of Blackheath. As you climb the hill the Dominican friary is on your right. At the crossroads in Blackheath look out for the unusual wooden signpost. **Turn R** and ride in the direction of Wonersh.

Carry on for nearly a mile along this narrow lane and **turn L** along Barnett Lane as you reach the outskirts of Wonersh. Cycle past houses and the large village green on your right.

At a T-junction **turn R** onto the B2128 and in a few yards **bear L** at the Grantley Arms, a 16th-century half-timbered inn. Keep the 'Pepperpot', as the locals call the picturesque bus shelter, on your right. Carry on down the hill to Bramley.

Cross over the mini-roundabout in Bramley village. For over 3 miles the route ahead is one of the most beautiful that Surrey can offer and is a

The crossroads in Blackheath

little-known gem. It runs past some beautiful houses and rolling parkland.

A detour may be taken at Thorncombe Street by **turning R** at the second turning. In about ¾ mile you reach Winkworth Arboretum, a National Trust hillside woodland of many rare trees and shrubs. In the spring the bluebells and azaleas are impressive and there are stunning colours in the autumn. There are two lakes and abundant wildlife. Bikes may be parked in the car park and you can walk to the higher levels past the end of the lake and perhaps sample the refreshments in the café at the top. There is an entrance fee. Return to Thorncombe Street by **turning L** out of the arboretum and **R** at Thorncombe Street.

In 1½ miles **turn L** in the direction of Gatestreet. In ½ mile, by a no through road sign, **turn R** along the private road which is also a bridleway. Watch out for the speed bumps. Follow the bridleway signs to the A281.

Turn R onto the A281 for about 200 yards. **Turn L** along the bridleway through Rooks Hill Farm. Just before the bridge **turn L** down the steps to the Downs Link. **Turn L** on the track. In just over ½ mile **turn R** just before a seat and planked bridge.

The shortened route joins here. Descend to a track and **turn R** to cross the canal and the river. Keep straight ahead up a few shallow steps to follow the narrow fenced bridleway through the fields to the end. **Turn R** at the T-junction and immediately **L** to Shamley Green. Stroll round the green and admire the setting, visit the Red Lion, perhaps for a pot of tea, and peep into the enticing delicatessen's, Poppys.

Having crossed the B2128 into Woodhill Lane, climb to the top of the wooded hill in the direction of Farley Green past some picturesque houses and farms. In about ¼ mile at a car park on the left there is a path leading to the ruins of a Roman temple where the ground plan has been laid out in stone.

Ride down a long gentle hill to Farley Green and **bear L** to Brook. In ½ mile **turn R** opposite Brook Farm, cycle under the railway bridge and into Little London. The William IV is on your left. There is a roaring log fire in winter and an inviting garden in the summer. At the T-junction **turn L**. In ½ mile **turn L** at the T-junction and the car park is soon to your left.

ALBURY

Albury lies by the Tillingbourne valley and the centre of the village is a conservation area. The village used to be by the church in the park but towards the end of the 18th century the owners enclosed the area and the villagers moved to the present site. The tall, ornamental chimneys were designed by Pugin and commissioned by Henry Drummond, an MP and banker. The excellent pub in the middle of the village is named after Henry Drummond. The village boasts three churches: the lovely old Saxon church in the park, the 19th-century parish church and the sectarian Catholic Apostolic Church. The Apostolic Church was closed following the death of the last administering member of an Apostolic College of twelve ministers as there was no-one left to appoint a new Minister.

WONERSH

The village used to be a centre of Surrey's cloth weaving industry. It is now an attractive village of half-timbered and tile-hung houses. Just past the village shop is the Wonersh Gallery where you can browse and see paintings, ceramics and sculpture. Further along the street to your left are the wrought-iron gates at the entrance to the park. Stroll along the path to find St John the Baptist church, part of which dates back to the 13th century.

12

Outwood, Haxted Mill, and South Godstone

23½ miles

This eastern side of Surrey is criss-crossed with motorways and main roads and yet you can find peaceful lanes and rural tranquillity. Pass Outwood Mill, the oldest windmill in working order in the country and Haxted Mill, a watermill on the River Eden with its bar and waterside restaurant. Climb Tilburstow Hill and see far reaching views across the Weald. Travel southwards past Prickloves Farm and South Park Farm along a scenic bridleway. Here is St Mark's Foundation, a religious and educational charity, where you may visit the Chapel and walk through the gate in the wall to an enchanting garden.

Map: OS Landranger 187 Dorking and Reigate (GR 327457).

Starting point: Outwood Common car park. Follow the A25 east from Redhill in the direction of Godstone. Turn right in Bletchingly by the Prince Albert pub in the direction of Smallfield. In about 3½ miles Outwood windmill appears on your left. Turn right almost opposite the windmill along a short track to Outwood Common where there is a free National Trust car park.

By train: Lingfield station is less than a mile from the route.

Refreshments: Haxted Mill Riverside Brasserie and Bar offers an inviting break for drinks by the mill race. Speciality seafood is available. The Fox and Hounds pub at Tilburstow Hill supports locally produced foods and prepares and cooks to order. The Bell at Outwood is round the corner from the windmill.

The route: Find the route easily between Haxted Mill and Tilburstow Hill by following the brown Surrey Cycleway signs for a distance of 8 miles. There is 4 miles of off-road riding, much of it on farm roads and tracks. There is more traffic on the B2028 for a mile or so and you cross the A22 but otherwise you use quiet roads. There are some climbs. To shorten the route start at Tilburstow Hill car park and leave out Outwood windmill. This will trim over 2 miles and a steep hill from the route.

From the car park, cross over the crossroads into Gayhouse Lane. Soon there are sweeping views over the Weald as you ride down to the T-junction. **Turn R** and you will pass St Mary the Virgin church at Horne. At a T-junction **turn L** and then shortly **R** into Bones Lane signposted to Lingfield and ride for just over 2 miles. This is level riding past fields. **Turn L** at the

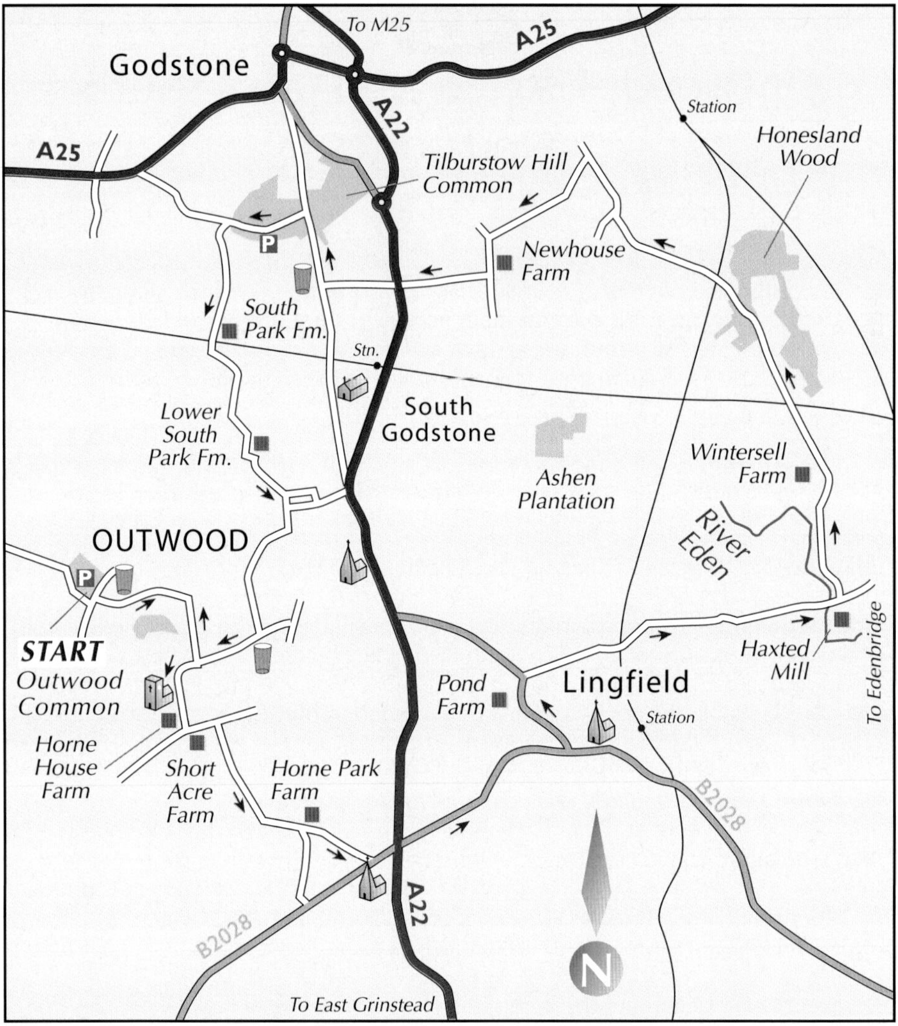

T-junction with the B2028 and cycle to a roundabout passing London Temple, belonging to the Mormon Church. Cross straight over and ride towards Lingfield.

As you enter Lingfield **turn L** at the mini-roundabout. In about ¾ mile **turn R** signposted Edenbridge. The views across the Weald gradually open out. In about 2¾ miles you will see Haxted Mill. The terrace by the mill race offers a uniquely beautiful spot to rest and have a drink. Browse in the mill museum next door.

From the mill, cycle up the short hill and **turn L** along Dwelly Lane. Here the route is on the Surrey Cycleway for 8 miles. You climb gradually on quiet lanes and you can see over the hedges to enjoy the views. You ride for 2 miles

The view from Tilburstow Hill

or so, over a railway bridge to a T-junction. Ignore the crossings on the way. **Bear R** and in a few yards **turn L**, signposted Hurst Green. Ride through Merle Common and in about 1½ miles **turn R** at the T-junction into Gibbs Brook Lane.

Turn L at the T-junction by Perrysfield Farm signposted to Tandridge. In 1¼ miles **turn R** into New Road signposted to Godstone (ignore the first right turn to Tandridge). **Turn R** at the T-junction and soon cross the busy A22. Cycle up the hill ahead and **turn R** at the T-junction and the Fox and Hounds pub is on your right. This is a good place for a rest. Climb Tilburstow Hill and **turn L** just over the brow of the hill into Rabies Heath Road.

About ⅓ mile from Tilburstow Hill car park watch carefully for a sign to Wychroft and South Park where you **turn L** by Snatts Hill House. The views are breathtaking as you glide downwards for a mile. Pass the entrance to Wychroft, a training centre for the Diocese of Southwark, pass Prickloaves Farm and go through a gateway with a private road sign and soon St Mark's Chapel is on the left, a haven of peace. In a few yards there is a door in the wall. Park your bike and walk through into an enchanting landscaped garden which is open to the public but you are likely to be alone.

Ride on to the gate and around it. Soon **bear L** on the concreted bridleway. The path narrows and you climb a hill. Near the top go through a gate. Leaving a concreted section barred by high gates **bear R** up a bridleway. Go through a gate at the top to Lower

South Park Farm. **Turn L** at the road and ride for ½ mile to a T-junction by a wooded residential estate. **Turn R** and in a few yards, by Brooklands, ride straight ahead through Hangdog Wood and past open fields for ¾ mile. After Tile Barn Farm walk or ride as the path narrows. At the gate **bear L** and climb the slope and then it is downhill to the road.

Turn R at the T-junction opposite the Jolly Farmer pub. **Turn R** in about ½ mile (unless you are cycling the shortened route and leaving out Outwood Mill) into Horne Court Hill and climb the hill that you rode down at the start of your ride. If you need to get off and push then glance to your right and savour the views. Soon you will see picturesque Outwood windmill on your right. The track to the car park is straight across the crossroads.

Outwood Post-mill

OUTWOOD POST-MILL

This is England's oldest existing windmill as it dates back to 1665. The mill makes an impressive sight with its 60 ft pair of sails. It is unusual in that it has been built with a single central trunk, hence the term post-mill. The entire mill chamber revolves around the post. It can be turned by a tail pole so that the sails may be faced to the wind. The mill is open in the afternoons from spring to autumn and there is a museum shop. Telephone: 01342 843644.

HAXTED MILL

Close to the Kent border is the interesting working watermill at Haxted next door to the Riverside Brasserie and Bar. Built of brick to the first floor with weatherboarding above, part of this is 17th-century, built on 14th-century foundations and part was built in 1794. It was always a corn mill and was last used for that purpose in 1945. The mill was opened to the public as a watermill museum and was the first of its type in Britain. The waterwheel operates machinery inside the museum and there is a collection of waterwheels, machinery and millstones, the wooden machinery and oak timbers being of considerable age. Telephone: 01732 865720.

13
Shackleford, Tilford and Puttenham

19½ miles

The route begins along pretty lanes towards Puttenham, passing through the attractive village of Shackleford. Ride along the Pilgrims' Way and on to Seale and the Manor Farm Craft Centre. Enjoy the tranquillity of Moor Park, a remarkably attractive residential area with interesting ups and downs on the outskirts of Farnham. Return either by Frensham Nurseries and the Rural Life Centre or you can choose to ride off-road. Cycle through Tilford with its village green and over the old bridge that crosses the rushing River Wey, eventually making your way to Cutmill Pond and back to Shackleford Heath.

Map: OS Landranger 186 Aldershot and Guildford (GR 935445).

Starting point: Shackleford Heath. Take the A3 southwards from Guildford and the exit to Hurtmore is in about 4 miles. Turn right to go underneath the A3 towards Elstead. Pass Shackleford church on your left and Shackleford Heath's woodland car park is about ⅓ mile on the right.

By train: Farnham Station is about 1½ miles from the route.

Refreshments: The Cyder House inn at Shackleford, the Good Intent at Puttenham, the Barley Mow at The Sands, and the Barley Mow at Tilford. For other refreshments try the Manor Farm Craft Centre and Frensham Nurseries Coffee Shop.

The route: This ride overlaps two or three miles of route 10 near Puttenham and route 16 near Tilford so if you have cycled those expect a sense of déjà vu. You can create your own mix and match combinations with these three rides. This circuit follows quiet lanes and one or two short stretches of off-road and B-roads. There are plenty of ups and downs but nothing too long or steep.

Turn R out of the car park. Ride down the short hill and **turn R** signposted Shackleford. Enjoy more downhill for ½ mile and pass the Cyder House as you enter Shackleford. **Bear L** into Hook Lane opposite the post-office in the direction of Puttenham. For 1½ miles you travel along one of Surrey's unusually open lanes. You may see fields of pigs on your right followed by a distant view of Puttenham Priory to your left. **Turn L** onto the B3000 and after the Harvester **turn L** and cycle through Puttenham village. The Good Intent is on your right. Try to leave time to stroll around the village which is very attractive and the haunt of artists.

From the end of the village it is nearly 2¼ miles to Seale. There is a long

The Manor Farm Craft Centre, Seale

downhill before the climb to the church and the delightful Manor Farm Craft Centre is round the corner in Wood Lane. The farm buildings have been converted into a tearoom which sells delicious cakes, has a craft shop, Artforge Jewellers and music room workshop. From the main route **turn L** along the Pilgrims' Way in the direction of Runfold for nearly ¾ mile.

Turn L into Binton Lane signposted to The Sands and climb the hill. In less than a mile, at the crossroads, **turn L** to detour to the Barley Mow pub where you can have a delicious baguette at a garden table on a sunny day.

Return to the crossroads and pedal up Botany Hill through some glorious woodland. In ½ mile **turn R** at the T-junction and in a few yards **turn L** into Compton Way, part of Moor Park estate. **Bear R**, remaining in Compton Way and ride the switchbacks. This is an exceptional residential area with some exquisite looking houses.

Ride down a steep hill from Moor Park passing the Constance Spry Flower School and over the River Wey. **Turn L** into Moor Park Way and in ¼ mile **turn R** into the B3001 for a few yards. **Turn L** into Monk's Walk and pass Waverley Court Farm, home of the Syon Limousin herd. Climb a hill and ride to the crossroads.

Go straight across into Lodge Hill Road and cycle for ¾ mile down the hill to the Farnham to Frensham road. **Turn L** into the A287 and immediately **L** again into Old Frensham Road riding past the recreation area.

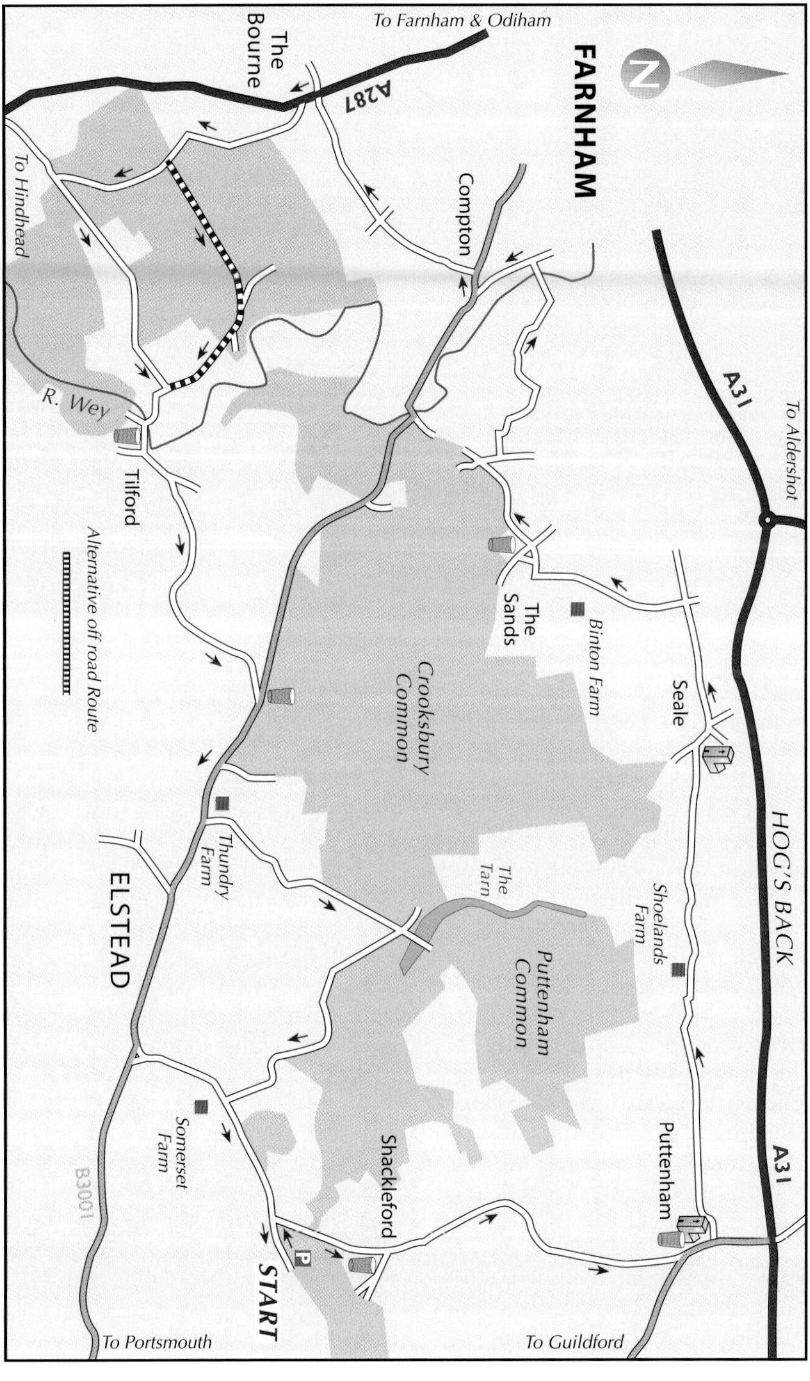

To Farnham & Odiham
FARNHAM
The Bourne
A287
Compton
To Hindhead
R. Wey
Tilford
Alternative off road Route
To Aldershot
A31
The Sands
Binton Farm
Seale
Crooksbury Common
HOG'S BACK
Thundry Farm
The Farm
Shoelands Farm
ELSTEAD
Puttenham Common
Somerset Farm
Shackleford
Puttenham
A31
B3001
START
To Portsmouth
To Guildford

Horses seen near Tilford

You can use an off-road route from the Old Frensham Road. Ride for nearly 1 mile along the Old Frensham Road to a short plateau between two downward slopes. **Turn L** for about a mile along an unmarked bridleway. The path runs through woods and then broadens out into a track. Follow the track round to the right and **bear L** to the Farnham to Tilford road round the barrier. **Turn R** to Tilford which is a mile away.

Otherwise, ride for 1½ miles along the Old Frensham Road and **turn L** at the T-junction into Reeds Road. You can enjoy visiting the Coffee Shop at Frensham Garden Centre and on the left the Rural Life Centre. **Turn R** to Tilford in 1¼ miles at the T-junction.

Cross the old bridge at Tilford over the River Wey and **turn L** to pass the Barley Mow. Tilford has a very attractive cricket green and on the north side is an oak thought to be well over 900 years old and 10 ft in diameter.

Cycle over the bridge beyond the Barley Mow. In ¼ mile **turn R** into Whitmead Lane. In just over 1 mile at the sharp bend by Whitmead House ride straight ahead into the bridleway. **Bear R** at the end onto the lane which slopes downwards past the Donkey pub. **Turn R** onto the B3001 for just over ¾ mile and watch carefully for Fulbrook Lane where you **turn L**.

This lane climbs gradually for just over a mile to Cutmill Pond. **Turn R** at the crossroads in the direction of Shackleford. In ¾ mile near the top of a rise **turn R** signposted Elstead. At the T-junction in another ¾ mile **turn L** signposted Hurtmore. Climb the hills and just over a mile further on

A summer's day at Tilford

Shackleford Heath car park is on the left.

PUTTENHAM

This is a picturesque village on the slopes of the Hog's Back, the cottages having been built over a period in the local materials of chalk and sandstone. The gates to Puttenham Priory are on your left at the start of the village. It was built in 1762, a fine example of a provincial Palladian house, but the best view is probably from the lane between Shackleford and the B3000. Sloping up to the Hog's Back is Duke's Farm, Surrey's last remaining hop garden. If you pass during the first three weeks in September it is said that the whole area takes on the aroma of hops. If you miss this you may find some compensation in finding Hop Garden Gold beer which is made exclusively from these hops.

SHACKLEFORD

The appeal of this village is that it is picturesque; the sandstone and brick houses are pretty and it has grown naturally. Stop for a moment opposite Aldro School and find the remarkable 18th century wall behind The Old Cottage. It is called a 'crinkle-crankle' wall, made of mellow brick and built in a series of bows to provide maximum weather protection.

THE RURAL LIFE CENTRE

This is a private collection marking over 150 years of farming. Aspects of rural life and local hop growing are displayed and a range of crafts are included. There is an arboretum and the Old Kiln Light Railway has preserved rolling stock, diesel and steam locomotives. There should be something of interest here for all the family. Telephone: 01252 795571 for details.

14

Holmbury St Mary and Oakwoodhill

17½ miles

Starting high in the Surrey Hills this ride takes you to the West Sussex border through deciduous woodland and pastureland where horses are much in evidence. Start at the picturesque Victorian village of Holmbury St Mary, visit the Church in the Woods at Oakwoodhill, the Hannah Peschar sculpture garden near Walliswood, some idyllic quiet lanes and the Sussex Border Path. There are some beautiful period houses and a good sprinkling of welcoming pubs.

Map: OS Landranger 187 Dorking and Reigate (GR 107442).

Starting point: Car park at The Glade, Holmbury St Mary. Take the A25 from Dorking. Turn left at Abinger Hammer onto the B2126. Turn right by the Royal Oak and the village green in Holmbury and the car park is at the end of the road at the base of Holmbury Hill.

By train: There are no stations very close to the route. The nearest are Gomshall and Ockley, both about 3 miles from the nearest point.

Refreshments: The Parrott at Forest Green, the Scarlett Arms at Walliswood, the Punch Bowl at Oakwoodhill, and the Royal Oak at Holmbury St Mary all offer refreshments. Try a weekend of cycling and stay at the well-known Holmbury St Mary Youth Hostel (telephone: 01306 730777) or at a village Bed and Breakfast.

The route: This ride is mainly on quiet roads with a short stretch of B-road and some easy off-road cycling. It has some ups and downs and there is a good climb to Holmbury St Mary at the end. To shorten the ride and to avoid the climb to Holmbury start the ride at the Parrott at Forest Green (ask before parking). To return: turn right onto the B2126 at the end of Plough Lane and ride for about 1¾ miles to the Parrott which is to your right.

Cycle from the car park in Holmbury back past the Royal Oak and the church. **Turn R** onto the B2126. From the Holmbury Garage continue pedalling for 2 miles downhill in the direction of Forest Green. **Turn R** at the T-junction in Forest Green and shortly **fork L** past the Parrot opposite the green. In less than ½ mile **turn L** just past McCann's Garage into a paved bridleway through a hidden gateway (ignore the footpath). The views unfold as you climb and Leith Hill is to your left. At the top you reach Gosterwood Manor Farm and then descend to a T-junction with Mole Street. **Turn R** and follow the lane for about 1¾ miles.

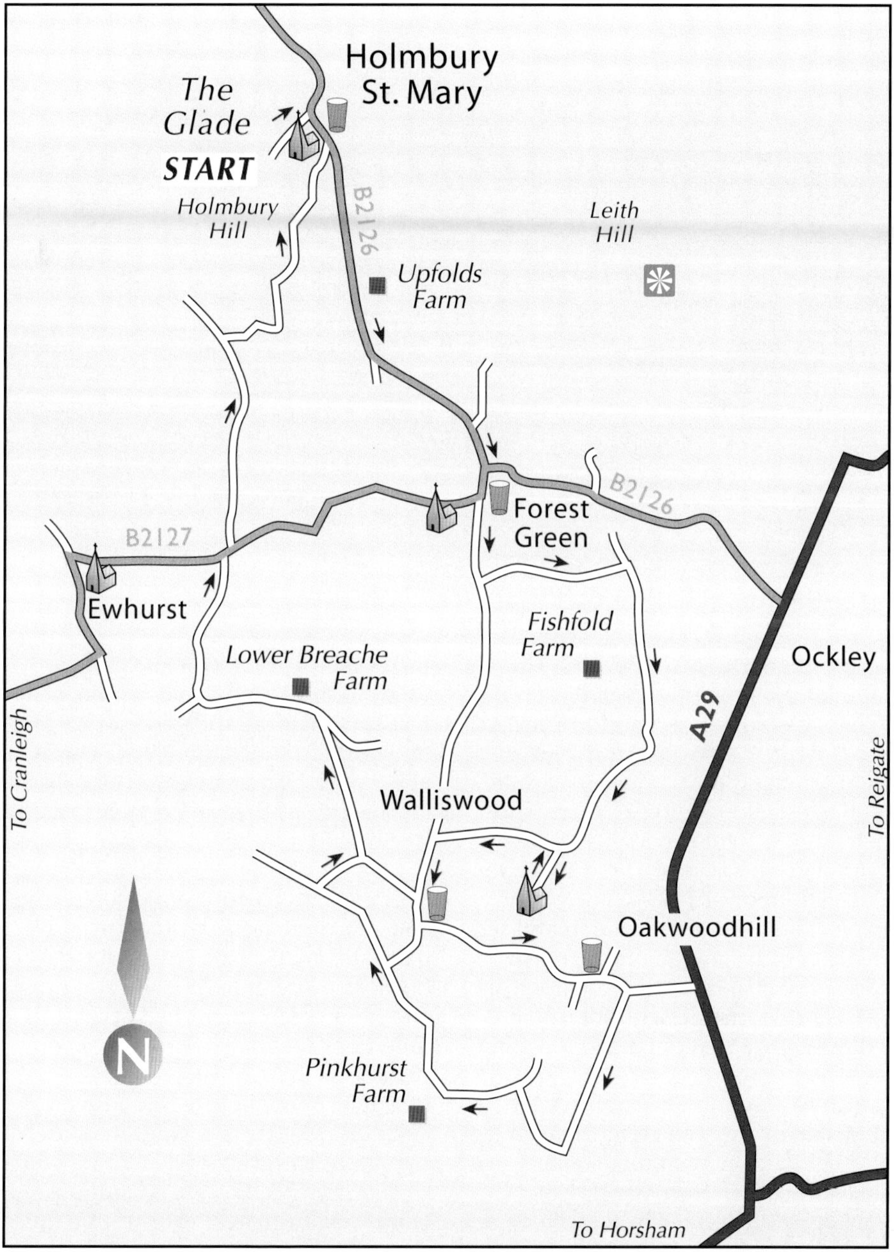

Holmbury St. Mary
The Glade
START
Holmbury Hill
B2126
Leith Hill
Upfolds Farm
B2126
Forest Green
B2127
Ewhurst
Fishfold Farm
Ockley
Lower Breache Farm
A29
To Cranleigh
To Reigate
Walliswood
Oakwoodhill
Pinkhurst Farm
To Horsham

The village church at Holmbury St Mary

Make a detour to Okewood Hill church, an older spelling of Oakwood. This lies straight ahead where Standon Lane bends right. Follow the lane down to the stream and push your bike up the short, steep slope to the 13th-century church of St John the Baptist in a clearing of the woods. There are various specimen trees such as mulberry and maple. Look inside the church and see the brass of de la Hale on the north side of the chancel in the old floor, six inches below the present one and protected by a sheet of glass.

Return to Standon Lane and **turn L**. Immediately on your right there is the Hannah Peschar Sculpture Garden. Cycle on past Gatton Manor Hotel to reach a T-junction. **Turn L** to the village of Walliswood. Shortly the Scarlett Arms pub is on your left.

In ¼ mile **turn L** in the direction of Oakwoodhill. In just over a mile, **bear L** at the junction, there is another pub on your left, the Punch Bowl. This is an atmospheric pub where you can also rest outside at the garden tables on a fine day.

In a few yards **turn R** down a steep hill and shortly **R** along a wide driveway, past Ruckman's. This beautiful large house is made of local stone and brick and is an enlargement by Lutyens. In ½ mile from the road, where the main path bears left, go straight ahead through the small gate signposted Sussex Border Path. A short middle section of path can have mud in winter so you may need to get off and push. Go through the next gate and up the slope to Monks Farm.

Turn R for nearly ½ mile along the Sussex Border Path, and the bridleway later becomes a wooded lane.

At the T-junction with Honeywood Lane **turn L** for nearly ½ mile and then **R** at the junction. Ride for 1¼ miles (ignoring the first turning to Walliswood) and **turn R** signposted Walliswood. In a few yards **turn L** onto a public byway and cycle under the arch of trees for over ¾ mile.

Turn L at the T-junction and ride along Lower Breache Lane. The road winds past houses and there are views of fields in all directions. Watch for Plough Farm, a beautiful house with a small lake on the left.

Turn R at the junction into pastoral Plough Lane and climb up and sail down past Yard Farm and up again to the B2127. **Turn R** and immediately **L** into Three Mile Road and climb gradually upwards for 1½ miles past scenic Lukyns Farm.

As the road bends to the left **turn R** around the base of Holmbury Hill towards the village along this winding lane through the trees, passing the University of London Mullard Space Laboratory on the way. **Fork L** on the outskirts of Holmbury down past the King's Head and continue downwards to the B2126. **Turn L** and **L** again at the green, go past the Royal Oak and **turn L** into The Glade and back to your car.

ST JOHN THE BAPTIST CHURCH, OKEWOOD HILL

In 1431 Edward de la Hale, accompanied by his son, set out to hunt wild boar near the church. The son fell from his horse into the path of a chased and wounded boar. Suddenly an arrow flew through the air, piercing the boar and saving the boy. Full of gratitude de la Hale vowed to devote a portion of his wealth to God and consequently the church was restored and enlarged.

THE HANNAH PESCHAR SCULPTURE GARDEN

This is a three acre sculpture garden fed by the waters of Standon Brook, in which modern sculptures and plants complement each other. Hannah Peschar is an enthusiast of modern sculpture and her husband is a landscape designer. There are landscaped pools and 80 sculptures are displayed. Telephone: 01306 627269 for opening hours.

FOREST GREEN FORGE

The Forge is housed in a picturesque, historic 16th-century building across the green from the Parrot Inn. Visit the Forge and Dragon Gallery where artist, James Davies, designs and produces handforged, unique ironwork. Examples of house and garden furniture, decorative artefacts and architectural work are on display. It is open Monday to Saturday from 8.30 am to 7 pm.

15

Leith Hill, Coldharbour, Ockley and Walliswood

14 miles

The ride starts on the slopes of Leith Hill, the highest point in south-east England, and curves around towards the hamlet of Coldharbour. See sweeping views of the Weald and South Downs as you descend towards Ockley. Cycle on to St Margaret's church which was almost rebuilt in the 19th century and Ockley Court with its attractive farm shop and flower nursery. Coast down Weare Street and up to the attractive Punch Bowl Pub at Oakwoodhill. Cycle along a bridleway and then climb Leith Hill along 'watery lane'. In spring and early summer, stroll through acres of azaleas and rhododendrons on the slopes of Leith Hill in the National Trust Rhododendron Wood.

Map: Landranger 187 Dorking and Reigate (GR 124413).

Starting point: (GR 147433) Park at the Landslip car park on the slopes of Leith Hill, near Coldharbour. Drive westwards along the A25 from Dorking. Pass through Westcott. Just over ½ mile past the Wotton Hatch pub turn left towards Leith Hill. In 3½ miles turn left in the direction of Coldharbour along Abinger Road. The Landslip car park is about a mile on your left but there are additional car parks nearby.

By train: Ockley Station is on the route.

Refreshments: Food and drink are available at the Punchbowl, Oakwoodhill, the Scarlett Arms, Walliswood, Ockley Court Farm Shop and the Parrot, Forest Green.

The route: There are some ups and downs and a long climb up to Leith Hill at the end of the ride but you can rest at the beautiful National Trust Rhododendron Wood near the top. The route is along undulating quiet lanes, a short stretch of bridleway and ½ mile on the A29.

Turn out of the Landslip car park in the direction of Coldharbour. The road winds up and down through beautiful countryside on the upper slopes of Leith Hill. In springtime the wild rhododendrons that line the road are a mass of purple flowers and in late April there are carpets of bluebells in the woodland. In about ⅓ mile **bear R** just before Christchurch, Coldharbour. The road slopes steeply for a few yards. **Turn R** again at the T-junction signposted to Ockley. Follow this road for about 1¾ miles to Stane Street as views to the South Downs spread before you. **Turn R** along the A29 in

the direction of Ockley for just over ½ mile.

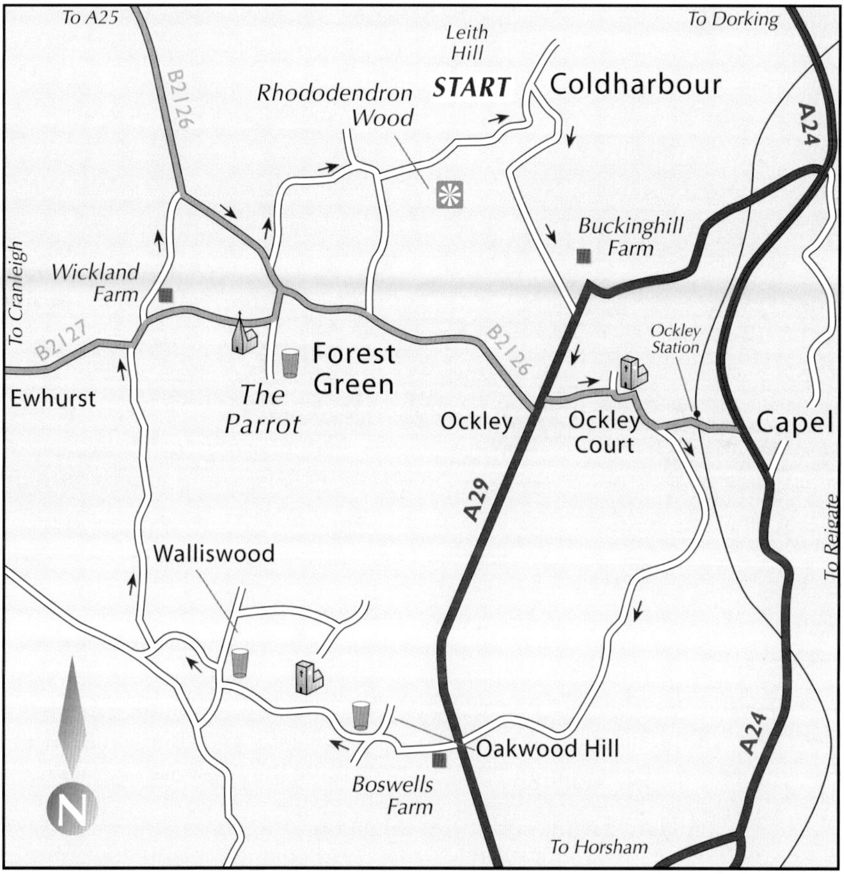

Turn L on the B2126 into Cole's Lane. In ½ mile you reach St Margaret's church almost rebuilt from a simple un-aisled sandstone building. On the right is Ockley Court Farm Shop bedecked with flowers for much of the year and inside is a small gift area, a varied range of foods and a flower nursery next door.

In about ⅓ mile **turn R** along Weare Street, signposted the Surrey Cycle Way. In ½ mile pass the entrance to Vann Lake on the right. Wend your way downwards through woodland and past fields for nearly 3 miles to Payne's Green.

At the crossroads go straight across the A29 and cycle past Boswells Farm which is on your left. Climb the hill and **turn L** at the T-junction. The Punch Bowl pub is soon on your right. This attractive pub is a good half way resting point.

Come out of the pub and **turn R** onto the road and then almost immediately **fork R** in the direction of Walliswood. In a little over a mile **turn R** at the T-junction towards the village.

The farm shop at Ockley Court Farm

Turn L in a few yards (before the Scarlet Arms) in the direction of Ewhurst. Cycle down the hill for just under ½ mile. Watch carefully for a public byway sign and **turn R** into it past the opening of the drive to The Pheasantry. The byway, Lowerhouse Lane, is used by horse riders.

Turn R at the T-junction into wooded Lyefield Lane. Watch out for wandering pheasants. Climb the short hill and near the end of the lane on your left is attractive, timber framed Cobbetts House. **Turn R** at the T-junction onto the B2127. Cycle up the incline and **bear L** at the top by the sharp right-hand bend. There are glimpses of Holmbury Hill to your left. In ¾ mile **turn R** at the T-junction onto the B2126.

In less than a mile **turn L** just past the brow of the hill into Tanhurst Lane, known locally as 'watery lane'. The reason for the name will become apparent to you as you climb ever higher up the slopes of Leith Hill. This is a challenging hill and you may decide to get off and push.

In a mile, at the top of the road, you will see the entrance to the National Trust Rhododendron Wood on your right. Leave time to stroll around this area particularly in springtime. It was given to the National Trust in 1945 by Dr Ralph Vaughan Williams, the composer, together with Leith Hill Place. Cycle the short distance to the off-set crossroads. Cross over the major road and take the way ahead in the direction of Coldharbour. There is still some climbing along this beautiful winding road. The Landslip car park is just over a mile from the cross roads.

LEITH HILL AND DR RALPH VAUGHAN WILLIAMS

Leith Hill is the highest point in the south of England at 965 feet and is owned by the National Trust. Walk up to the top and there is a folly, the top of which reaches to 1,000 feet. Vaughan Williams, the composer and prime mover in the creation of the Leith Hill Festival, lived for many years at Leith Hill Place on the slopes of Leith Hill. He donated both that and the Rhododendron Wood to the National Trust in 1945.

VANN LAKE

This is a nature reserve owned by the Surrey Wildlife Trust (telephone: 01483 488055) from whom a nature trail guide can be obtained. The lake covers 8 acres and is an old hammer pond originally created by damming a stream which flows on to be the Arun. There are some unusual deciduous trees around the lake and many varieties of fungi.

Bluebells carpet the slopes of Leith Hill in spring

16

Tilford, Frensham and Alice Holt Forest

17 miles

A village green, the River Wey, Frensham Ponds and Alice Holt Woodland Park make this a glorious ride over ever-changing countryside. See the Wey meandering around the large green at Tilford, ride across Frensham Common to Little Pond with its attractive beach where swans cluster. Detour to the village of Frensham and then on to the Great Pond. Ride along lanes to Alice Holt Woodland Park where there are cycle tracks in the ancient forest. Emerge at Rowledge and treat yourself to refreshment at the attractive Cherry Tree pub. Ride through the village of Millbridge and perhaps make a visit to the Rural Life Centre on your return to Tilford.

Maps: OS Landranger 186 Aldershot and Guildford (GR 873434), and Alice Holt Woodland Park Map, free from the Woodland Centre.

Starting point: The car park by the river at Tilford village green. Tilford is about 1½ miles south-west of the Milford to Farmham road, the B3001.

By train: Bentley station is 2 miles from the route.

Refreshments: The Barley Mow, Tilford, dated at 1730 is reputed to be the second oldest pub in England and has a resident ghost. Alternatively try the Forest Centre at Alice Holt, or the Cherry Tree pub in Rowledge. There are also pubs at Millbridge, and a coffee shop at Frensham Garden Centre.

The route: Country roads, lanes, bridleway and cycle tracks at Alice Holt, with ¼ mile on the A287. Only small undulations apart from the gradual climb to Alice Holt. If you want to visit the Rural Life Centre at Reeds Road, Tilford, telephone: 01252 795571 for opening times.

Turn L from the car park and climb the short rise to Tilford Road. **Turn L** in the direction of Hindhead. Ride past pines and paddocks for 1¼ miles and after the sign for Rushmoor **turn R** into Grange Road.

In about a mile you reach a ford which is a bit too deep for most cyclists. There are planks where you can push your bike across. As you climb the rise you will see Frensham Little Pond on your left, a beautiful area to stop and wander. The beach is bounded by pines, reeds wave in the breeze and there is abundant wildlife. Cycle on the winding road as it becomes Priory Lane and the attractive Old Post House is on the corner.

Turn L onto the Frensham Road, the A287, and pedal up the hill for ¼ mile.

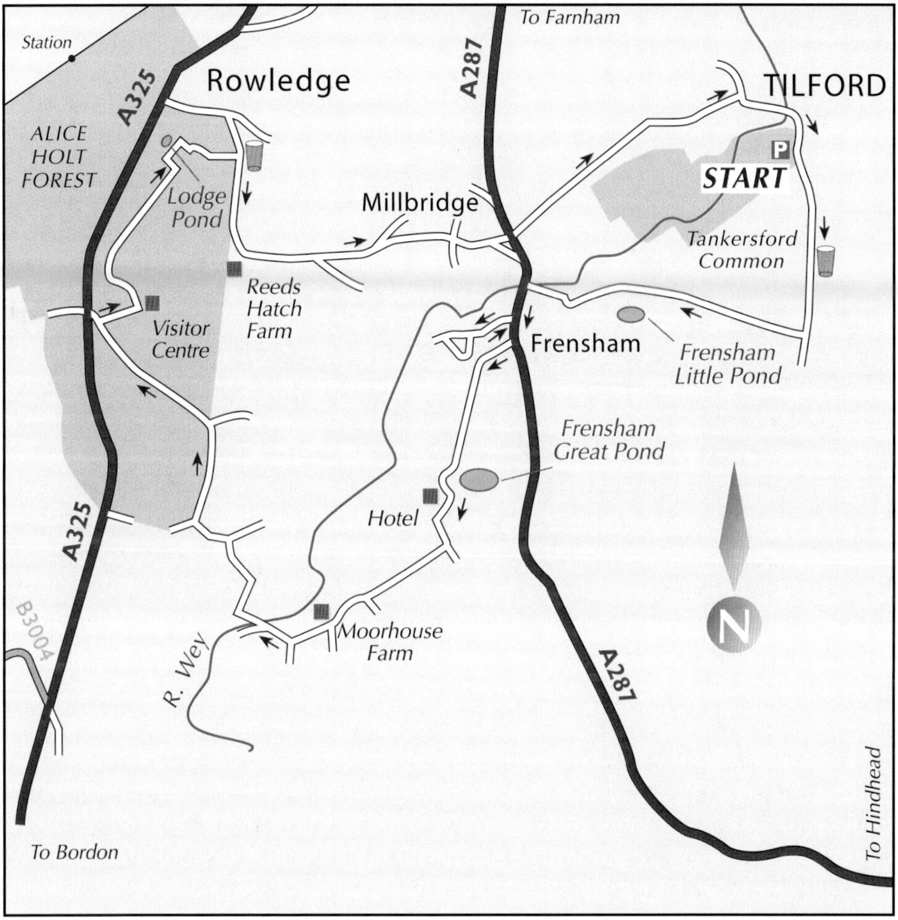

At the green you can **turn R** to make a detour of a mile to Frensham village to see the cottages, and St Mary's church which has a massive three-legged copper cauldron at the back of the north aisle. Legend associates this with a witch who inhabited a cave near Waverly Abbey. Return to the green and the A287. **Turn R** immediately into Bacon Lane. Cycle along this tree-lined road backed with fields down to Frensham Great Pond and the Frensham Pond Hotel.

Continue on Bacon Lane, pedal into Hampshire and keep turning right! In detail, follow the road as it bends sharply to the right and becomes Frensham Lane. At the T-junction **turn R** into Wishanger and **R** again into Frensham Road and down the hill past some attractive houses. **Turn first R** and then **R** again across the bridge into Heath Hill Lane signposted to Dockenfield and Bentley. Rest at the bridge and watch the River Wey as it flows on to Tilford. Cycle on past open fields and a pretty cottage to climb the shaded hill and back into Surrey.

Picnicking by the river at Tilford

Turn L at the T-junction into Old Lane and as you ride along you will see long views to the Downs on your left. After a short distance **turn R** at the T-junction and climb High Thicket Road. Continue climbing and **bear L** following the road past the turning to Dockenfield.

Forestland is on your left and in about a mile there is a sign to Alice Holt Woodland Park owned by the Forestry Commission. **Turn R** here and cycle along the drive and around the barrier to the Forest Centre. You have an opportunity to sample the coffee whilst you check the Lodge Pond cycle route to Rowledge on the free map available at the Centre. If you stray from the marked route the map should help.

Return to the barrier, **turn R** at the grassy triangle and then **bear L** along the cycle track to Lodge Pond. Follow the wide stony track which has posts with green cycle logos to indicate the way. **Bear R** as the path climbs and **R** again at a seat following the signs. **Turn L** opposite a viewpoint. Ride past fir trees and a grassy area to Lodge Pond.

The path bends sharply to the right. At the T-junction **turn L**. In a further ¼ mile **turn L** away from the cycleway at a cross-paths. Go along the footpath for about ⅓ mile to the car park and Rowledge. St James' church is just to the left. **Turn R** out of the car park and the Cherry Tree pub comes into view. This is a welcoming pub and the cherry tree provides a wonderful shady haven on a warm day. Watch for the tree of charities on the wall.

Continue on and **turn R** at the

T-junction into Boundary Road. Cycle down the hill parallel to Alice Holt Park and in ½ mile just before the bottom **turn L** signposted Millbridge. Cycle along this narrow lane and soon there is a stream running past, attractive houses and an old oast house.

Fork R into peaceful Broomfield Lane, cross straight over at the crossroads and immediately **turn L** at the British Legion Hut towards Millbridge. There is another pub on your left and later you pass the end of an unusually named street, ' Wire Cut'. Cross over the A287 and ride through past the picturesque houses of Millbridge.

Bear L to Reeds Road which is about 1½ miles long. You can visit the Frensham Garden Centre on your right where there is a coffee shop or the Rural Life Centre, close by on the left-hand side, a private collection of 150 years of farming.

Turn R at the T-junction and back to Tilford passing over one of the pair of bridges over the River Wey. **Bear L** just before the village green. The Barley Mow pub is on your left and the car park is by the river on the right.

ALICE HOLT WOODLAND PARK

This park which is an ancient forest has many claims to fame, from supplying oak for the replica of the Globe Theatre in London to supplying timber for Britain's naval fleets in the past. It is now managed for the Forestry Commission as a working forest and as a park for visitors and wildlife. Pick up a leaflet at the Forest Centre for details and read about the Purple Emperor butterfly.

FRENSHAM COUNTRY PARK

The Great and Little Ponds were created in the Middle Ages as stewponds to provide fish for the palace of the Bishop of Winchester and his household at Farnham Castle. It is now an important wildlife conservation area owned by the National Trust covering an area of 1,000 acres and well known for good bird-watching, sailing, fishing, walking and safe beaches.

17

Newdigate, Charlwood, Gatwick and Rusper

19 miles

Surrounded by main roads and within a stone's throw of Gatwick Airport you enter an island of rural calm riding along leafy lanes and over tracks past attractive farms and pastureland. The Six Bells pub in Newdigate is reputed to have been a smuggler's haunt with underground passages where contraband French brandy, wine and silk were stored. Consider a visit to Gatwick Zoo and Aviaries or Lowfield Heath windmill. See an interesting corner of Newdigate and, if you are in luck, experience the thrill of jets thundering towards you at the end of the Gatwick runway. Cycle along peaceful country lanes to the village of Rusper and past moated Cudworth Manor as you return.

Map: OS Landranger 187 Dorking and Reigate (GR 197420).

Starting point: The Six Bells pub at Newdigate. Drive southwards from Dorking on the A24. Turn left at Holmwood immediately past the Duke's Head. At a T-junction in Newdigate turn right and the Six Bells is shortly on your right opposite the church. Please inform the landlord before leaving your car (telephone: 01306 631571).

By train: Crawley station is 2 miles from the route.

Refreshments: The Six Bells, Newdigate Newsagents for snacks and sandwiches, the Half Moon at Charlwood, the Lamb's Inn at Lambs Green and the Star at Rusper.

The route: There are quiet, and a few busier, country lanes as well as off-road riding. It is an undulating ride but the hills are short. In wet weather avoid a 300 yard section of potentially soggy bridleway by turning left from the Six Bells car park. Follow the road past the Surrey Oaks pub as it changes name from Cidermill Road to Partridge Lane. Just over 4 miles from the Six Bells turn left into Charlwood Lane and join the route at paragraph three below.

From the Six Bells cross the Rusper Road and pass St Peter's church on your left. Ride for ½ mile along Church Road to a sharp left-hand bend. **Turn R** into Cudworth Lane and then soon **turn R** along a private road and bridleway, to Green Lane Farm. Pass the farm buildings and a telephone box and then go through a gate and past landscaped ponds. Go through another gate and the surfaced bridleway ends abruptly part way through the field.

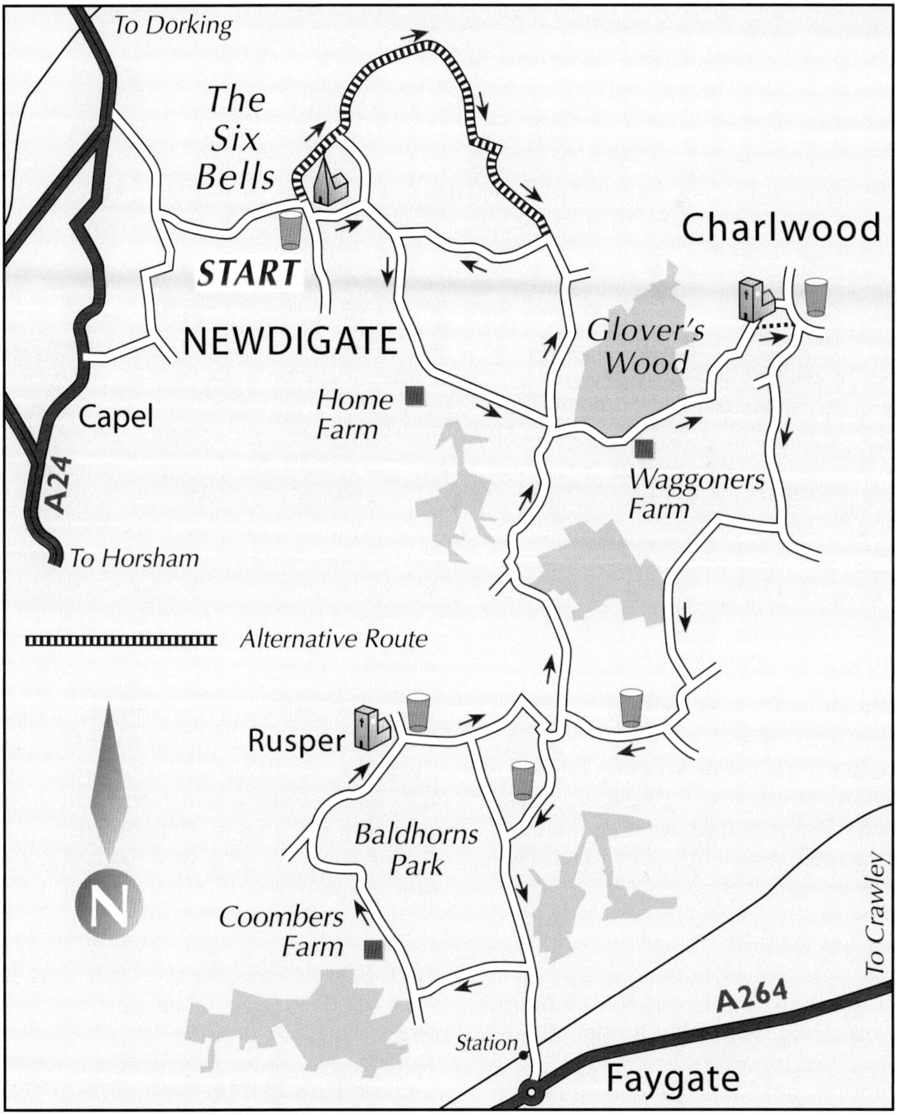

To Dorking
The Six Bells
START
NEWDIGATE
Charlwood
Glover's Wood
Home Farm
Capel
A24
Waggoners Farm
To Horsham
Alternative Route
Rusper
Baldhorns Park
Coombers Farm
To Crawley
A264
Station
Faygate

For about 300 yards you may need to get off and push your bike after wet weather as you cross the field and pass through two gates.

Turn L onto the driveway and immediately **fork L** onto a track past a lone pine. Home Farm is on your right.

Cross a bridge and notice the spillway between the two lakes to the right and left. The track rises gradually. Turn to see views of the North Downs from the rise. **Turn R** at the T-junction into Cidermill Road and in a few yards **turn L** into Russ Hill.

The starting point of the ride

The alternative route joins here. Gatwick Zoo is on your left in about 1¼ miles. Consider strolling around the ten acres of landscaped grounds where you will see birds, butterflies, small mammals and many rare plants. There is an entrance fee. An 18th-century windmill is also on the site having been moved from Lowfield Heath.

In less than ¼ mile watch for a narrow footpath on your right by the pillar-box. It is opposite Glovers Road. Push your bike and visit the church of St Nicholas which dates back to early Norman times. Look for the screen across the south chapel with carvings of dragons, griffins and angels, which is thought to be the finest piece of medieval woodwork in Surrey. Continue along the footpath and you arrive at an attractive corner of Charlwood with the Half Moon pub and some pretty cottages on your right. Ride to the T-junction and **turn R**. **Turn R** again signposted to Ifield, opposite the newsagent's. In about a mile you pass near to the end of the Gatwick runway. Pull into the lay-by and see planes with headlights blazing take off and roar overhead.

Turn R in just over ¼ mile, cycle into Prestwood and pass Water Hall and Hillybarn Farm, home of the Hookwood Pointers. Cycle down the hill and **turn R** at the T-junction signposted to Ifield. **Turn R** again at the next T-junction into Rusper Road.

In ¾ mile **turn L** in the direction of Lambs Green. Shortly there is the Lambs Inn. **Turn L** at the T-junction into Faygate Lane and pass Amberley Manor.

In little more than ¾ mile **turn R** at a cross-lanes signposted to Wimlands. Ride along the quiet lane for a little over ½ mile past North Grange Farm. At the T-junction **turn R** signposted to Rusper.

In about ¾ mile there is a sharp turn to the left. Consider making a short detour for about 300 yards along the driveway and bridleway to your right to glimpse Baldhorns Park, a beautiful house with a small lake.

Continue on the main route to the T-junction. **Turn R** along Horsham Road and pedal for about a mile. You reach the village of Rusper and the Star pub is on the right-hand corner. This attractive 15th-century pub has an inglenook fireplace and a priest hole as well as home-cooked food.

Turn R at this corner in the direction of Faygate and cycle down the hill. **Turn L** in about ½ mile at a sharp right-hand bend. In ¾ mile, by a cottage, **turn L** along Longhurst Lane and at the top of the hill **bear L** into Orltons Lane.

Turn R at a T-junction into Partridge Lane and you will soon recognise a few yards of the route which you rode over on your outward journey.

In a little over 2 miles watch out carefully for Burnt Oak Lane and **turn L**. This is a somewhat potholed road to Cudworth. Moated Cudworth Manor is in ½ mile. It has an attractive roofed bridge with a dovecote and part of the Manor dates back to the 13th century. **Bear R** at the end and you join the outward route. **Turn L** at the T-junction and Newdigate church is shortly on your right. Cross to the Six Bells.

ST NICHOLAS CHURCH, CHARLWOOD

There are wall paintings on the south wall which were recently restored. One dates from the 13th century and is a strip cartoon of the life of St Margaret of Antioch, and a 14th-century painting is of three kings hunting, who encountered three skeletons. Visit the church, see the paintings and the medieval screen and read a self-guiding sheet to fill in the fascinating detail.

NEWDIGATE

The name comes from 'On Ewood Gate' which means on the way to the yew wood. This was one of the old iron villages of the Weald. Iron working reached its heyday in the 16th century and with larger blast furnaces enormous amounts of wood were required. The main works were at Ewood, north of the village and were owned by the Earls of Warenne. Their forebears founded St Peter's church in the 12th century as a hunter's chapel, used by Norman hunting parties when they hunted in the Wealden forest.

18

Dunsfold, Chiddingfold and Hambledon

19½ miles

This ride which starts at Witley station is along some delightfully quiet lanes past woodland, pastureland and some fine country houses. There are wide vistas of Wealden countryside and views to Blackdown. Cycle through the village of Hambledon and along a tranquil bridleway to the 13th-century Dunsfold church and the Holy Well, where the water was reputed to have healing powers. At Shillinglee Park you pass what is said to be the best nine-hole golf course in the country. Pass the hamlet of Gospel Green and ride along idyllic lanes to explore the pretty village of Chiddingfold. This is the largest of the 'fold' villages and was a glass-making centre in medieval times.

Map: OS Landranger 186 Aldershot & Guildford (GR 949379).

Starting point: Witley station. Drive south on the A3 from Guildford and take the Milford exit. Turn second left after the traffic lights and at the roundabout take the A283 exit in the direction of Chiddingfold. In just under 3 miles turn right immediately after the railway bridge. Witley station is on your right after the Wood Pigeon pub. There is a parking charge. Alternatively the ride can be started in Chiddingfold or Dunsfold where parking is possible on the roads alongside both of the greens.

By train: Witley station

Refreshments: The Sun, Dunsfold and the Crown Inn, Chiddingfold, a hotel and restaurant.

The route: This is quiet and for the most part uses lanes where you will see very little traffic, except on the B2131 where traffic is faster. There are some ups and downs but the hills are short. To shorten the ride: turn left at the signpost past Combe Court and save 2½ miles by leaving out Chiddingfold. Return to Witley station which is just over 1½ miles away.

From Witley station cross over at the crossroads and cycle into New Road. In ½ mile cross straight over the A283 and ride into Lane End in the direction of Hambledon.

In less than ½ mile **turn R** into Vann Lane towards Hambledon village where there is a post-office and attractive village green. Follow the lane and **bear L** in ¾ mile at the sharp bend by Placewood Farm. This is a pretty winding lane which drifts gently downwards at the start.

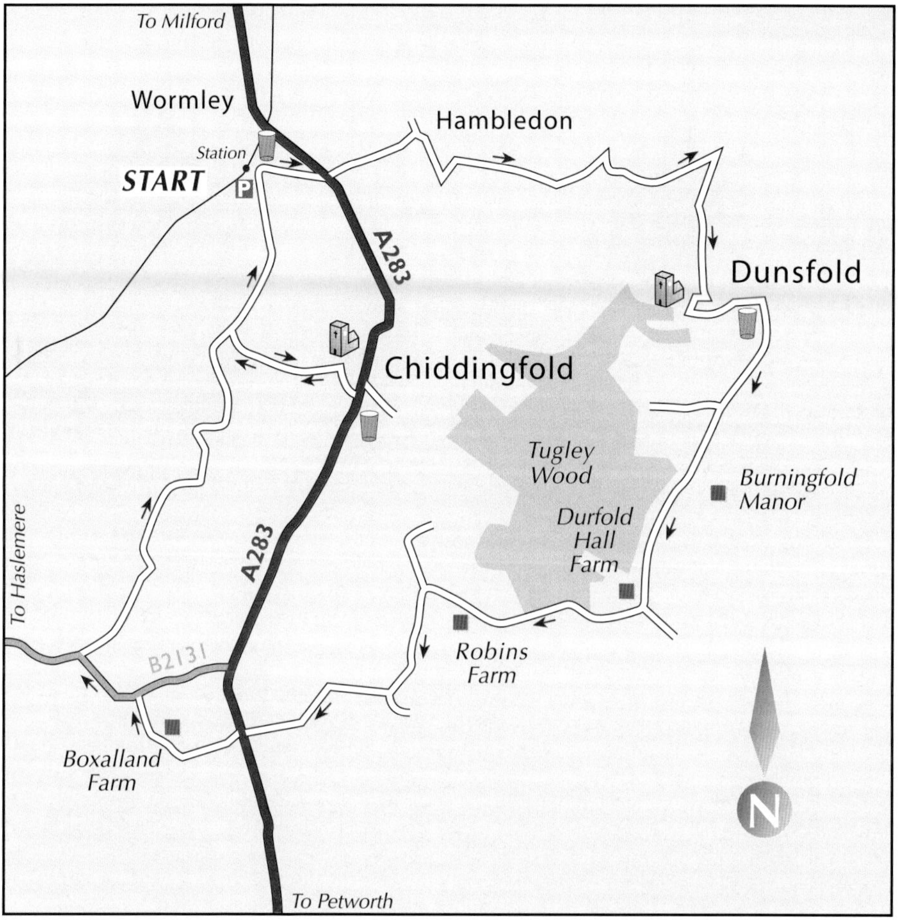

In a further mile follow the road as it bends sharply right. Ignoring the turning to Upper Vann, **turn L** almost immediately along the drive/bridleway to Burgate Farm. This is a delightful ride as the way bends through countryside with open vistas. Hurtwood and Hascombe Hill can be seen to your left and views across the Weald to your right. The drive becomes a stony track which emerges opposite Gorebridge House near Loxhill. **Turn R** into quiet Hookhouse Road and ride in the direction of Dunsfold church.

Turn R in a mile to make a loop to Dunsfold church. It is unusual in that it is ½ mile away from the village amongst some attractive 17th-century houses. As the church dates largely from the 13th century and has some fascinating features it is well worth visiting. The Holy Well is 100 yards down a footpath to your left just before entering the churchyard.

Follow the road downwards from the church. **Turn R** at the T-junction with Hookhouse Road and pedal up the short hill. **Turn R** at the T-junction in

Chiddingfold's attractive village pond

Dunsfold and look out for the Sun pub on your right. There are tables spread out over the green and it is a good place to rest, eat and drink. See the towering oak whose girth is said to be 20 ft.

Continue cycling across Dunsfold Common in the direction of Chiddingfold, passing the war memorial on your left. Ride for ½ mile down the hill and then **turn L** up a rise in the direction of Plaistow. Pedal for 1½ miles passing Burningfold Manor far to your left, a large 15th and 16th-century timbered building, and climb to Durfold Farm. Just past a telephone box **turn R** into tranquil Fisher Lane in the direction of Chiddingfold. **Turn L** in a further 1½ miles in the direction of Shillinglee. Climb the short, sharp hill and Shillinglee Park Golf Club is on the left. **Turn R** at the T-junction by Shillinglee Home Farm and ride for 1¼ miles to the crossroads with the A283 and cross straight over.

From the hamlet of Gospel Green ride up the hill in the direction of Haslemere. **Turn L** at the T-junction onto the B2131. In ½ mile **turn R** in the direction of Killinghurst along this quiet and undulating lane, one of Surrey's gems. In ¾ mile **turn L** into West End Lane signposted to Chiddingfold. Pass the duckpond and cycle on past fields and through woodland for 2 miles, climbing Pook Hill to a T-junction. **Turn R** in the direction of Chiddingfold. Notice Combe Court Farm across the fields on your left. This picturesque building has multiple gables and a circular tile-hung turret. In ½ mile the way divides at a signpost. Left goes to Witley station directly and right takes you on the detour to Chiddingfold.

Turn R to Chiddingfold and follow the road ahead (ignoring a sign to turn left). Ride downhill past a residential area and in a mile **turn R** at the T-junction into the village. There are pretty tile-hung cottages and the early medieval Crown Inn is opposite the church of St Mary. Having rested in Chiddingfold, retrace the way you entered the village and rejoin the main route. Cycle into Coxcombe Lane and then **turn L** into Ridgeley Road and up the hill, retracing your way. Go straight ahead and Witley station is about 2¾ miles away. The car park is to your left before you reach the Wood Pigeon.

CHIDDINGFOLD

In the 13th century, Chiddingfold was an important centre for the glass-making industry and employed skilled craftsmen from northern Europe. It continued for four centuries until the use of Wealden timber for fuel was forbidden. It was from the village industry that glass was provided for Westminster Abbey and for the royal chapel at Windsor Castle. In St Mary's church there is a window made out of many fragments of glass said to have been dug from the remains of the three Chiddingfold glass furnaces.

DUNSFOLD

The church of St Mary and All Saints is one of the highlights of Dunsfold. It is ½ mile from the village and dates back to the 13th century. It is one of the few churches in the area that has remained virtually unchanged. People who lived in the surrounding farms built the pews in 1300, most of which remain. Look out for the impressive millennium tapestry at the west end of the church, embroidered by the people of Dunsfold.

19

Alfold, Loxwood and Cranleigh

18 miles

Beginning near Alfold Countryways Experience, you ride past idyllic-looking cottages, through Sidney Wood on the Wey South Path and reach the village of Alfold with its tiny green, St Nicholas' church and the Crown pub. Dip into West Sussex at Loxwood and follow part of the towpath of the Wey and Arun Canal which runs from the Thames to the Channel. Return via Tisman's Common to Cranleigh and have a drink at the Cromwell Coffee House. Cycle back along a farm track to a bridleway by the Arun Junction Canal.

Maps: OS Landranger 186 Aldershot and Guildford and 187 Dorking and Reigate (GR 028352).

Starting point: Sidney Wood near Alfold, a concealed Forestry Commission car park. Follow the A281 Horsham Road from Guildford and at Alfold Crossways turn right and immediately right again in the direction of Dunsfold, following the signs to Countryways Experience. In about a mile slow down as you pass the lane to Countryways Experience. In just over 1/10 mile turn left along an unmarked metalled lane. Drive along the lane which becomes a track and the car park is on your right.

By train: There is no railway station close to this route.

Refreshments: The Crown at Alfold, the Onslow Arms at Loxwood with a garden by the canal, the Mucky Duck at Tisman's Common where you can play outdoor chess, and the Compasses at Laker's Green all offer refreshments. The Cromwell Coffee House, Cranleigh serves meals and snacks all day. You can sit outside under umbrellas and people-watch.

The route: Includes many quiet lanes, bridleways, woodland tracks and a canal towpath. There is the one significant hill, Crooks Hill, but none too long or steep. Take care crossing the A281 Guildford to Horsham road.

From the car park follow the track back to the Alfold to Dunsfold road and **turn L**. In about a mile **turn L** along Ram's Lane signposted to Knightons. The next 2½ miles offers some idyllic cycling along quiet lanes and tracks. Ride past pretty Ram's Cottage and past paddocks to the T-junction. **Turn L** into Knighton's Lane. Cycle down a steep hill, over a stream and climb the next hill.

Ride straight ahead for a little over ½ mile from the point where the road

changes to a woodland track (ignoring crossing tracks). This is part of the narrowing Wey South Path through Sidney Wood. **Turn L** at a metalled road by stables into Rosemary Lane. There are some very attractive cottage-style houses as you wend your way to Alfold. At the entrance to the church notice the picturesque cottages and watch for the stocks. Go inside and see one of the oldest and best preserved fonts in Surrey.

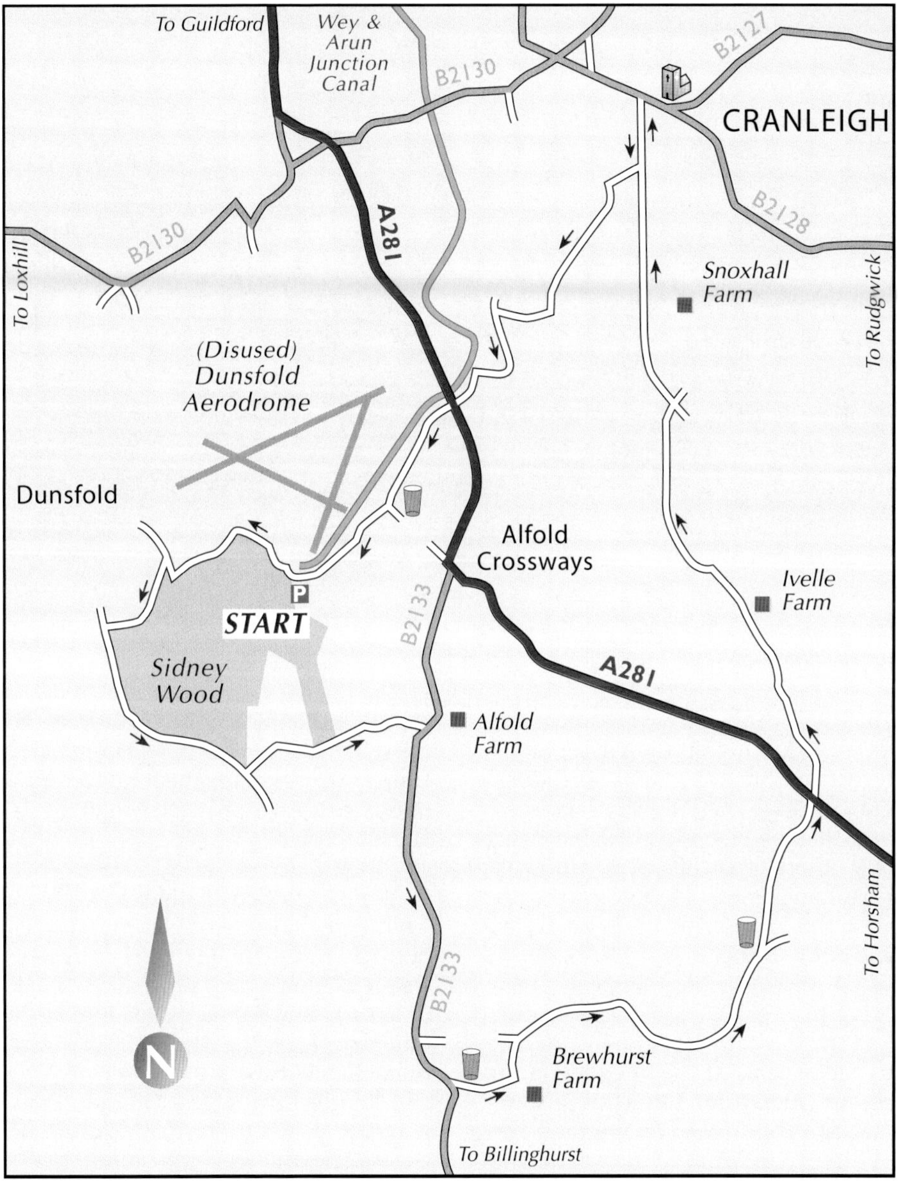

The Cromwell Coffee House, Cranleigh

Turn R onto the B2133 for about 2½ miles. Ride through the village of Loxwood where there is a post office. **Turn L** along the Wey South Path immediately before the Onslow Arms pub. Alternatively, if you are in need of refreshment rest at a table on the attractive lawns of the pub by the Wey and Arun Canal.

It is a peaceful ½ mile stretch of canal and the towpath is narrow so give way to pedestrians. At the bridge try a short detour. **Turn R** for 100 yards or so to see attractive houses on your left and a mill on your right. Return to the bridge over the canal and cross it, continuing on the bridleway to a junction with the road where you pass through a gate.

Turn R at the T-junction and cycle along the Loxwood Road which is not busy but may have some fast traffic. In about a mile the Mucky Duck pub is to the left. **Turn L** here along Hornshill Lane as it rises gradually for another mile. Cross the A281, the Guildford to Horsham road.

Alternative off-road route to Cranleigh: This is away from traffic but it can have muddy patches in wet weather. Climb Cooks Hill and after ¾ mile **turn R** at Baynards Road. In ½ mile **turn L** off the road and immediately **turn R** to the Downs Link and Thurlow Arms. The Thurlow Arms pub is to your left. Baynards station is ahead. The old station, first built in 1865 is now privately owned but has been beautifully restored. Keeping the station to your right ride along the Downs Link, the disused railway line from Shalford to Shoreham. Follow this for 4 miles to rejoin the route at Knowle Lane.

St Nicholas' church, Alfold

Otherwise, climb Cooks Hill and pedal along Knowle Lane for nearly 4 miles to Cranleigh. (You will return as far as Oaklands on the way back.) The Cromwell Coffee House is across the High Street and to your right. The cricket green and some of the older attractive houses are along the High Street to your left. Consider parking your bike to explore the village.

When you have explored Cranleigh turn into Knowle Lane (the road on which you entered Cranleigh). In ½ mile **turn R** into a bridleway opposite Oaklands, just past Knowle Park Nursing Home. Ride down and then up an incline and on along the farm road past Holdhurst Farm. **Turn L** at the T-junction into Alfold Road for over ½ mile.

Cross straight over the A281 Guildford to Horsham road, and take the Wey South Path directly opposite. Follow the grassy path, go through a wooded area by the Wey and Arun Junction Canal and over a firm field to Laker's Green. You will see the Three Compasses pub a few yards ahead. This used to be on the way to now-disused Dunsfold Aerodrome. **Turn L** for a few yards to the T-junction and then **turn R** in the direction of Dunsfold. The Countryways Experience is about ½ mile further on to your left.

CRANLEIGH

Cranleigh has the reputation of being the largest village in England. It has a cricket green with attractive houses round two sides of it and Cranleigh School is nearby. At the other end of the village is an obelisk which was built in 1794 to commemorate a turnpike which was opened between Guildford and Horsham. There is also an Arts Centre nearby. If you prefer to watch the world go by, just sit under an umbrella at the Cromwell Coffee House.

THE WEY AND ARUN CANAL

The canal was originally completed in 1816 but fell into disuse following the coming of the railways. It is now being restored to reopen the link between the Thames and the 23-mile canal to the Channel, and to create wildlife habitats along the canal corridor. Working parties offer their time but further restoration depends upon the goodwill of landowners and support from the public. A leaflet can usually be found by the towpath at the Onslow Arms.

THE COUNTRYWAYS EXPERIENCE

This estate has sections that are likely to appeal to various age groups. There is a family farm, a farm museum, a Victorian walled garden and a farm shop. The walled garden which has been worked for one hundred years produces flowers and fresh vegetables for the shop. More recently ex-merchant seamen have been trained for a new career in gardening there. For opening times, telephone: 01403 753589.

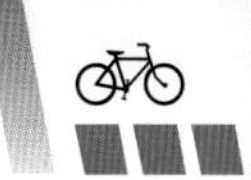

20

Baynards, Barns Green and The Downs Link

21 miles

This route should be particularly easy to follow, the return ride being on the Downs Link. It starts at Rudgwick on the Surrey/West Sussex border and crosses the county boundary to reveal glimpses of the Weald and the South Downs. Cycle along tranquil lanes past fields, cottages and Lannards Fine Arts Gallery to Barns Green. Pass the Bax Castle pub and on to the Downs Link to ride past Christ's Hospital School playing fields. Perhaps you may treat yourself to a cream tea if you pass Slinfold on a Sunday. At the end the route continues along the Downs Link to Baynards, a restored Victorian station. Carpets of bluebells await you in late April.

Maps: OS Landranger 187 Dorking and Reigate, or Explorer 134 Crawley and Horsham (GR 090343).

Starting point: The car park at the King's Head pub, Rudgwick. Take the Guildford to Horsham road, the A281. Turn left at Bucks Green onto the B2128 through Rudgwick. Drive up through the village for about a mile and the King's Head is on your right. The car park is immediately opposite but ask, or telephone the pub first (01403 822200). They are open from 11 am all day and Sundays from 12 noon.

By train: Christ's Hospital station is less than ½ mile from the route.

Refreshments: Apart from the King's Head, you can stop at the Blue Ship at The Haven, the Queen's Head at Barns Green or the Bax Castle by the Downs Link. Slindon Church Hall offers cream teas on a Sunday. The Thurlow Arms at Baynards produces its own brew real ale (telephone: 01403 822459).

The route: There are some gentle ups and downs but it is an easy ride and returns along the disused railway track, the Downs Link. It is a quiet route with the only significant exception being ½ mile on the A29. Here you can push your bicycle on the pavement.

Turn R out of the car park and ride down the hill for a mile through the village of Rudgwick . At the T-junction **turn R** onto the A281 for about 200 yards and then **L** into Haven Road signposted to the Haven. In less than a mile at the top of a long rise **turn R** signposted to Garlands. This is an idyllic lane flanked by verges. You cycle past fields and a cottage or two. At a

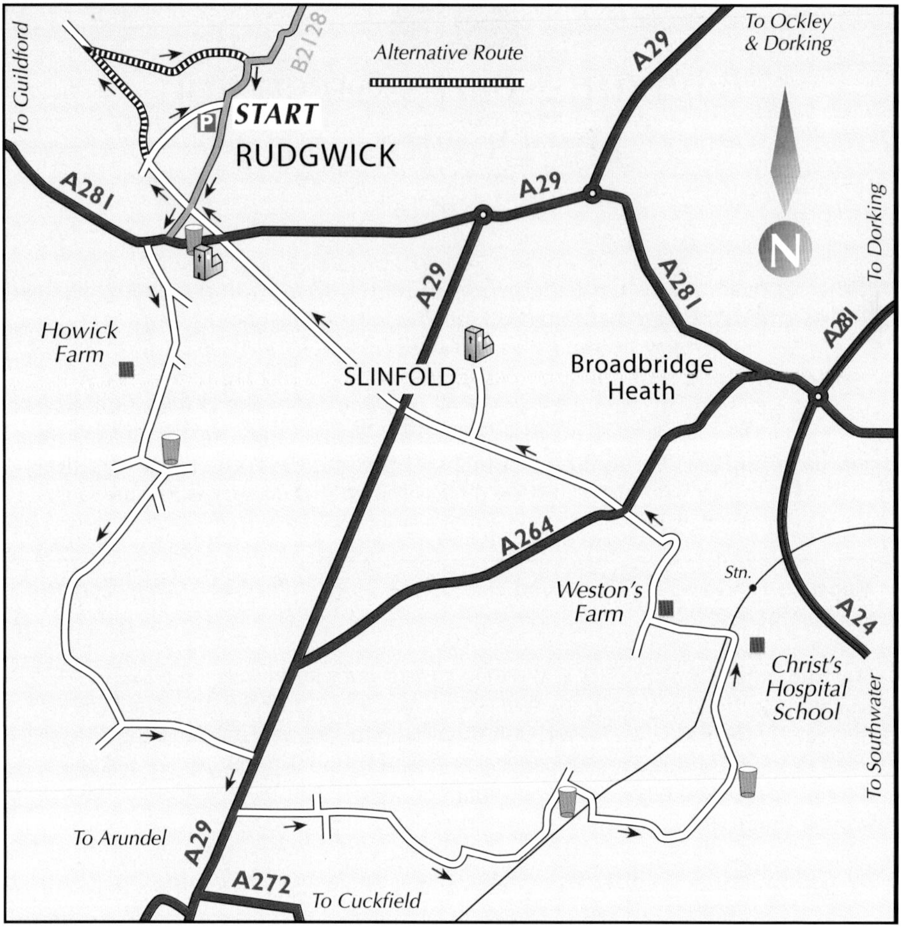

T-junction **turn L**, signposted to The Haven.

Soon the Blue Ship pub is on your left. It is an attractive country pub with climbing roses and cottage flowers. There are several small rooms inside, one with photos of Newfoundland dogs and the prizes that they have won. From the route **turn R** into Okehurst Lane. Enjoy some wonderful open views to the South Downs across the Weald. In about 2¼ miles **turn L** just after a group of cottages. In a further mile you reach the A29, Stane Street, having passed Lannards, a gallery, on your left. Stane Street was the course of the old Roman road from Chichester to London.

Cross the A29 and **turn R**. It is recommended that you push your bike on the pavement for less than ½ mile, past Sotheby's Auction Rooms, to avoid riding on the narrow busy road. **Turn L** into New Road and in 1½ miles **turn R** and then **L** at offset crossroads in the direction of Barns Green. Ride for a

On the Downs Link near Rudgwick

mile, cycling down the hill and **bear L** away from the level crossing. Soon you see a shop and the Queen's Head on your right. This is about halfway and makes a good place to stop and rest.

Cycle to the green, **turn R** into Two Mile Ash Road and ride under the railway line. Climb the gradually sloping winding road for 1½ miles. **Turn L** over a bridge and immediately **R** to pass in front of the Bax Castle pub. This is an alternative place to stop right by the Downs Link. Ride on to the far side of the car park, through a small gate and **turn R** onto the Downs Link.

Follow the course of the old railway track for ¾ mile and **turn L** onto the driveway past the playing fields of Christ's Hospital School. Following the Downs Link signs: ride to the road just outside the gates of the school, **turn L** and go over the railway bridge. At the T-junction **turn R** and in about ½ mile just before a bend **turn R** again. Cycle up the slope and opposite double wire gates make a sharp turning to your **L**. You are back on the old rail track where there are wonderful open views.

In 1½ miles cross a minor road and look to see if St Peter's church has a poster advertising Sunday cream teas. If you are in luck **turn R** and cycle for ½ mile to Slinfold church hall. Then return to the track by pushing your bike through the gate. In ¼ mile **bear L** on the track keeping close to the houses. After riding under the A29 the Downs Link runs on a ridge above the surrounding countryside. Look downwards to see trees below you and in 1½ miles the River Arun as it runs beneath the bridge. Go through the gate and cross the A281. Cross to the offset path the other side to pick up the track. In less than ½ mile ride under Rudgwick bridge. Cycle for ⅓ mile further and ride under Lynwick Street Bridge.

If you do not want to go on to Baynards, you can make your way back to the car park from here. Join the road by cycling a further 200 yards, **turn L** and go through a five-bar gate by Woodsomes Farm. **Turn L** into the concrete lane to Lynwick Street. **Turn L** over the bridge and ride past the brickworks and up the last short sharp hill to Church Street. **Turn R** and the King's Head and the car park are in a few yards.

To go to Baynards, from Lynwick Street Bridge continue along the Link track. Climb a steep hill, Downs Link Bridleway, **bear R** at the top and ride down to a road. **Turn R** over the bridge and make your way down the slope to pass beneath it. On the Downs Link go through a gate to Baynards station and the Thurlow Arms pub. Retrace your way to the last bridge, climb the rise to the road and **turn R** into Cox Green Road. Ride for a mile to a T-junction. **Turn R** into the B2128 and the car park is ½ mile on your right.

THE DOWNS LINK

The bridleway was established to link the North Downs Way and South Downs national trails. The trail crosses the Low Weald and follows two former railway lines for about 38 miles. One was from Guildford to Christ's Hospital and the other Itchingfield Junction, near Christ's Hospital, to Shoreham-by-Sea. Both were closed in 1966. The restored station at Baynards was built in 1865 and is now privately owned.

Baynards station

BAYNARDS BLUEBELLS

If you cycle the end of this route towards the end of April you can expect to see carpets of bluebells in the woods. You could even park your bike and venture along one of the many footpaths on foot to see even more.